Yellowstone Moose Droppings

Yellowstone Moose Droppings

William J. Lewis

Cover art by Margaret Bach

ISBN 978-1-4583-1092-7

Table of Contents

Prologue

Suzanne Kusserow, my wife

Since Bill and I have been going to Yellowstone National Park for many summers (he for 50, I for 25), it seemed not only appropriate but endearingly necessary, as a wife and co-worker, to add a prologue and chronology to what has been such a fruitful relationship between us and Yellowstone.

Each summer, we came as early as his other job--a professor of communication at the University of Vermont--would allow. We would arrive in May just before the vacationers started pouring in, along with other seasoned teachers from colleges and universities around the country. And each year a new crop of naturalists-to-be joined us all, with degrees in geology, environmental science, or biology, the ink still fresh on the parchment.

Two days of classes began: developments of the last year, budgets, the new wolf pack spreading out of the Park boundaries, assignments to various parts of the Park, new rules and regulations, a wolverine study underway, greetings from the Superintendent, statistics on the size and health of the bison and elk herds. Then followed two days of exploration of the Park for the new hires, by bus. I always eagerly anticipated these trips. Bill knew not only the skills of teaching and effective personal communication, he also knew history, geology, and flora and fauna, as well as the personality of each burping mud pot, geyser, and boiling hot spring. So the trips were a magical information trove of facts, beauty, camaraderie, recognition, and pride in working in one of the premier parks of the world. The cadre of new National Park Service interpreters included (at various times): a high school science teacher from Kansas; a young woman who was transferring from Denali National Park, now learning about elk instead of caribou; a

German woman who was exchanging her work in a park at home for a summer in Yellowstone; and a couple from Oregon--she a librarian who would be working in the Visitors' Center Book Store, and he would be driving a tour bus.

I saw hidden gems in the Park's necklace of jewels. We followed a hot brook far off the trail to its beginning: a bubbling, frothing spring circled by yellow monkey flowers. We went far past crowded Artist's Point at the Lower Falls of the Canyon of the Yellowstone to get a less- obstructed look at the narrow, sudden depth of the canyon, the river visible far below as a silvery thread in the sunshine. And, of course, we reviewed safety tips. We learned on a walk how to gauge the amount of time for stops to view an unusual plant or bird as well as to give people breathing time at 7,000 foot elevation in the thin, mountain air.

We were all absorbing, almost invisibly and osmotically, how Bill taught. For him, learning, sharing, and teaching were all part of an intricate daily pattern. For example, he would say, "Look, I don't remember this plant from last year … seems like a new location for a pink monkey flower. Anyone have a Shaw's wildflower guide with them?" Or, another time, "Let's just stop in this beautiful place and sit still and listen. We don't use quiet often enough; probably because we aren't comfortable with silence. Let's try it!" Later, we discussed how we and our visitors might react to sitting quietly for a while. We agreed it sets up a more "wondering" tone and pace, a good thing (but also shouldn't be too long, as people get restless).

On another hike, a visitor asked me, "Why are those trees planted so close together?" How might *you* reply? "Nature doesn't obey rules?" Would you launch into an explanation of how the serotinous cones of the lodgepole pine are opened by the extreme heat of a forest fire and then scatter seeds profusely wherever there is a little sunlight? "Remember," Bill would say, "there is no such thing as a foolish question … just one for which someone needs a simple answer. People have different past experiences and perspectives and see the same phenomenon differently. Try this: ask a group of people to close their eyes and react to the word "tree". You will have responses ranging from maple, olive, ponderosa pine, cypress, and northern spruce, depending on where each person is from."

And of course there was the irresistible fun and mystery of waiting for a geyser eruption. Some liked to predict the exact time of the eruption. Bill might say, "Here we are at Grand Geyser. It last erupted at 8:15 a.m. and lasted 20 minutes with three separate eruptions. Here are some predictive clues. Is the water rising and holding in the pool? Is it bubbling? Vent Geyser, adjacent to Grand, went off less than 20 seconds ago. Vent and Grand Geysers are connected underground, as some geysers are. Let's wander around and hear people's comments. And see that group huddled together against the rain on the edges of the pool? They're geyser gazers, and they gather every summer to monitor their favorite geysers. They know these geysers well. They can be very helpful to you in answering questions."

During these pre-season training days, we stopped at dark and ate together in the employees' dining room, then bunked out in dorms or tents. The next day was more of the same, which of course, with nature's exuberance, is never the same. And that evening, it was back to our assigned locations to unpack, prepare slide talks (now PowerPoint!), shorten uniform pants, and settle in.

On work days during the summer Bill was dressed as a tourist in order to observe interpreters undetected. He could usually maintain his anonymity. Accompanying naturalists new and old, he went on all-day hikes up Avalanche Peak, ate lunch on the Petrified Forest walk, tagged along on Terrace Walks at Mammoth Hot Springs, and sat through evening campfire talks. He took reminder notes on microscopic pieces of paper so that he remained almost invisible as a critiquer. The occasional naturalist would lure him out of hiding: "Bill, I don't remember the name of this plant. Isn't it the one the retired pharmacist told us he used to make into a lotion to treat lice?" (Answer: Larkspur)

After a hike he would sit down with the interpreter and give him or her suggestions on how to be more effective in reaching people and in sharing their enthusiasm. For example, one day a new interpreter was giving a short walk along the edge of 1200 foot

Yellowstone Canyon. After viewing the magnificence of the Falls he led his group along the rim of the Canyon. The drop to the river was dramatic and dangerously steep, and stunted trees and minarets of harder rock accented the straight slide down. Sitting on a log after the visitors had dispersed, Bill said to the naturalist, "The three older women in your group really didn't hear much of what you were saying. You were right on the edge of the ravine and they were sure you were going to topple backwards down into the river. The trick to giving a good talk is not only imparting information. It's having the ability to observe what is getting absorbed and what is not, and why."

Once on a day off we started to climb Electric Peak in the early morning darkness to make it up and back in daylight. Bill got hypothermic when the relentless wind whipped across the talus slope near the top. His voice started to slur and the gorp I carried with me as a sneaky treat became a lifesaver as we huddled behind a rock, leeward of the wind. Another day we balanced on logs to get near enough to a pale yellow water lily to smell its subtle scent. I learned how not to fish, instead catching sagebrush, the overhanging limb of a Douglas Fir and Bill's hat. And of course we tried to predict Steamboat Geyser. It became an example of the mysteries that surrounded us. It delighted and confounded by remaining a mystery, despite Bill's curiosity and indefatigable data-collecting. No one ever did successfully predict Steamboat; it thankfully continues to elude human hypotheses.

Bill is treasured by many of the interpreters he trained, some as long as 30 to 40 years ago. We make shorter visits nowadays, which are pleasantly punctuated with: "Hi Bill! Welcome back! Do you remember the time …?" In the midst of the splendor and excitement in Yellowstone, Bill was there, effusing, sharing, informing, challenging. His approach was to help people discover things for themselves, which is usually the best way. True to his orientation, he wrote this book with an interpretive slant. He has always been concerned that the arrow (facts) when sent by the bow (communication skills) will truly hit the target (us) so we can appreciate Yellowstone all the more. His factual knowledge of the

Park was inspired by his joy at its eternal splendor and quixotic leaps into different moods. We sincerely hope that this book of remembrances will entertain and inform you, the reader, about this remarkable place and Bill's experiences there for over half a century.

Introduction

I include here for the reader some background about who I am, how I came to do this work and how my career developed. A more detailed autobiography is included in Appendix A.

I began my teaching career in 1948 at Ohio University as an instructor in dramatic art and speech. This left my summers free. Since I grew up in Idaho within a few hours of Yellowstone, I was familiar with that area and loved it. So in 1949 I started at Yellowstone as a Seasonal Park Ranger in law enforcement and, after three years, became a Seasonal Park Ranger-Interpreter. Interpretation is the process of helping a person see, hear about and experience a new place in a meaningful way. At Old Faithful Geyser, for example, an interpreter would explain to park visitors why a geyser erupts, what Old Faithful's particular geological history is and how humans have interacted with it over time.

After a few years I began teaching interpreters. This summer job was a great complement to my teaching during the rest of the year; I could teach communication in both an experiential and an academic setting. Subsequently I was on the faculties of Penn State University and the University of Vermont, teaching speech, communication, and sociology.

One summer Steamboat Geyser suddenly became much more active and became the world's highest geyser. More and more people began visiting it, so I was sent to supervise interpretation at the Norris Geyser Basin, where it was located. Steamboat, though it had no predictability, did give a fabulous warning. The first bursts were like the sound of a jet engine taking off at full bore. Echinus Geyser, also at Norris, began erupting on a frequent predictable schedule, spurting from a deep blue pool surrounded by a rim of light brown spines resembling an echinoderm, a spiny sea urchin.

The volume of visitors was huge, and I organized staff and visitors so people could get as much out of the experience as possible.

Several summers later I was put in charge of the interpretive staff at Old Faithful Geyser, one of the most well-known geysers in the world. Here I broadened and deepened my knowledge of Old Faithful, in particular, and geysers in general. I learned to acutely observe and to record minute, dissociated data. After several summers my predictions were much more accurate. Sharing this with the interpretive staff was also more and more rewarding every year.

One spring, because of summer commitments at the University of Vermont, I discovered with dismay I could spend only three weeks at Yellowstone. What was I going to do for only three weeks? Could they use me for such a short period? Could I keep my job there? It turned out that the chief of interpretation at Yellowstone liked the training I had given the staff at Old Faithful Geyser during previous summers. He had the novel idea to use me for three weeks to observe interpreters in the field giving presentations to the public, followed by a one-on-one critique of their communication skills. I became "Oral Communication Specialist" for the park for many summers after that. So, something I thought was a misfortune turned out to be a turning point for my career.

There was another fortuitous event. When the NPS national office learned what was going on with training in Yellowstone, they investigated and decided to adopt it nationwide. They liked the idea of combining didactic learning with on-the-spot critiquing of an interpreter. This led to my writing a training manual for interpreters, *Interpreting for Park Visitors*, (1980) that is still used currently for training and is in print in several languages. In addition, I was videotaped doing interpretive training with individuals and groups in many settings, and the resulting video, "The Process of Interpretive Critiquing," has been widely used for trainings throughout the United States, England and Canada. I was also invited to give trainings in person in national parks in most of the 50 states as well as in parks in Canada and England.

The completion of these projects in the late 1970s coincided with growing concern in the U.S. about the rapidly dwindling supply of energy in the world. Energy conservation and alternative energy development were new ideas at the time, and some believed they were critical to the survival of civilization. The core values of the NPS were preservation of natural resources and maintenance of ecological balance. It seemed it could and should play a role in fostering attitude change about energy consumption. The NPS administrators, aware that I had a sabbatical leave coming up and had free time, asked me to take on a new task. They contracted with me to gather information about how to interpret energy issues to the public. This would be a refreshing "updating" of the information and the approach traditionally used by interpreters, and I was glad to do it. I embarked on an eight-month tour of 71 parks, forest areas, and museums in the U.S. and Canada, traveling by truck fitted out with a camper in the back. I collected great energy interpretation ideas already in use in parks for possible use nationally and made wide-ranging suggestions about how to present ideas to the public. I also identified negative attitudes among park staff to promoting energy conservation. I inventoried each park's energy and resource use and looked at (what are known today as) sustainability practices so the parks could practice what they preach. These included such things as promoting shuttle buses instead of personal vehicles, composting toilets, green building construction, recycling, and non-motorized use of the backcountry.

These memories and many others have made me realize what a rich experience I've had in my 50 summers working in Yellowstone and other parks. I wrote this book to share some of my stories with you. My perspective can be readily observed by the reader to be influenced by my work as an interpreter of nature to the public and my interest in human communication. To provide a broader picture than I could alone, I asked several of my family members to write chapters, which they have graciously done and these are credited to them.

Chapter 1

Moose Droppings

On the slopes of Dunraven Peak in central Yellowstone National Park I was giving a guided walk one day. The goal was to encourage visitors to use all their senses to become acquainted with plants. I was showing the group how the animals were very careful not to overgraze an area. They grazed at one place for a few moments and then moved on to another. A woman in the group wanted to know what animal had been grazing there. I told her and the group that it was probably a moose and showed her how the vegetation had been grabbed and torn, not severed, as other foraging animals do. Her response was that it couldn't have been a moose because everyone knows that the habitat of a moose is a lake, a pond, or a marshy area. I assured her that moose are sometimes found on mountainsides, but she was unconvinced.

Someone then brought some scat to me for identification. I explained to the group that its shape and size indicated that it was most likely moose scat. "But," my disbeliever insisted, "moose live in lakes, ponds, and marshy areas." "Sometimes they live on mountainsides," I countered. A little further on someone found some hair, which I explained was from a moose. I showed how the hair was hollow, how its airspace provides insulation to keep the moose warm in the extreme winters. This time, the doubting woman shook her head in silence, perhaps wondering why Yellowstone interpreters weren't given better training.

Later, as the group knelt around a patch of flowers to smell them better, I looked up and saw a bull moose come over the brow of a hill not more than 50 feet behind my group. I asked the woman if she'd believe that moose sometimes graze mountainsides if I showed her one. "Of course," she asserted. "Then please turn around and look," I invited. By the time she turned, two more bulls had appeared. All three stood there observing the group as the woman seemed to swoon and sway at the sight.

My wish is that all interpreters might have such an "on-cue" experience.

Chapter 2

Bears Aware

In 1928 when I first visited Yellowstone National Park as a five year old with my parents, bears were frequently seen along the roads begging for handouts from people. They were also turning over garbage cans in the campgrounds, sniffing tents to find food and eating garbage at the bear-feeding spectacle arranged for park visitors in the evenings. A park ranger sat astride his horse and narrated while visitors sitting in bleachers observed the frenzy. First, trucks emptied a large pile of odoriferous garbage. Then out of the woods came a large number of black bears who began stuffing themselves. After a short time, the grizzlies began to arrive. Their arrival scattered the black bears and quickly reduced the piles of garbage to zero; then they ambled away, fat and satisfied. Park visitors were also satiated, even though the "show" was not good for the bears. Instead of seeing wild bears foraging for food in a natural setting, people saw bears who were habituated to "people's" food: Twinkies, cellophane wrappers, mustard-soaked hamburger. It was a great show, and some older people who revisit Yellowstone today regret its closure.

As you can imagine, this change of wild bears to beggar bears caused many problems. Bears began to establish "territories" along park roads where they stopped cars to beg. As one car stopped to feed a bear, the cars behind stopped to see what was going on and to take their turn at providing "goodies" and taking pictures. On the narrow roads of the Park you had no way to move in either direction, and these "bear jams" took hours to sort out. It was at one of these bear jams where one park visitor had what he described to me as a "terrifying experience." I was working as a park ranger at the Old Faithful Visitor Center desk when this man came rushing up to me in a panic. His face was scratched and bleeding and he held in his hand a badly-broken pair of eyeglasses. "Oh, I've just had the most terrible experience! I saw this bear by the side of the road. I wanted to see it up close so I stopped, threw it a cookie, reached for my camera and began taking his picture. One cookie wasn't enough I guess because he poked his nose inside the car, sniffing away. I didn't know what to do, trapped behind the steering wheel. Then I remembered that at home when my dog got too close I'd blow on his nose and he'd back off. So, I blew on the bear's nose and he reached his paw into the car and scratched me across my face and broke my glasses!" I wanted to remind him dogs and bears are not the same, and that what's good for a dog is not necessarily good for a bear, but I deemed it unwise to give him a "lesson". I commiserated with him and referred him to the resident doctor at the Old Faithful Inn. Later that summer I ran across another bear jam and I wasn't nearly as restrained. I was patrolling in the Old Faithful area and I parked my patrol car at the edge of the road and walked ahead to see what was going on. The first thing I saw was a small black bear trying to climb in through one of the back windows of a car. Apparently there was some food on the back seat. I walked to the driver's window and said, "Sir, there's a bear trying to climb in your back window. I suggest you roll it up." Without turning to see that I was a park ranger in uniform, he put his finger to his lip and whispered, "Yes, we know. We're going to take him home for a pet." Then he looked to see the source of the voice he heard and I gave him a stern reprimand and explanation of his foolishness.

When a Clark's Nutcracker, often called the camp-robber bird, grabs our morning muffin and flies to a nearby branch chattering loudly, that is both annoying and amusing. Grizzlies on the other hand are often seen as negative creatures, nosing around back-country campsites waiting to squash our food caches and tents with a swipe of their huge paws. Such a difference in size does justify caution and fear. Yet, grizzlies, too, are fighting for their lives in this increasingly human ecosystem. One day while driving to the northern part of the park near Mt. Holmes, I was delighted by the rare sight of two young brother grizzlies playing together. Of course I was alerted by the large number of cars nearly blocking the road. The bears were seemingly unaware of the excitement they were causing, rolling over in the grass, 'dancing' through the green meadow, cuffing each other with mammoth paws ending in nails as long as one's fingers. One was tinged copper and light brown; the other the 'standard' darker color. They were ignoring their job of tearing up spring beauty plants to get at the tender roots and hunting patches of huckleberries (bears are about 80 percent vegetarian). It was a lovely summer day, and they decided to play … although such roughhousing, as in most young animals, is preparation for the serious stuff later on. As a park ranger, I had to keep people from wandering too close, but we were all delighting in watching this clumsy dance by creatures that were seldom seen playing, let alone seen at all! Finally, they ambled down to the river, the awkward 'pigeon-toed' placement of front paws belying the fact that they can run in bursts at 35 miles per hour. It was a wonderful glimpse into another side of a grizzly's life that those visitors and I will long remember.

Chapter 3

Do You See What I See?

How many sheep will the Empire State Building hold? Do you think this is a trick question? When I have asked my students at the University of Vermont this question, I receive answers like: "It can't hold any sheep because it doesn't have any arms," or "3,141,252," or "It depends on whether they've been fed recently," or "It depends on whether they've been sheared recently or not," or "None, because there's a city ordinance against this sort of thing." These answers suggest the idea: "Ask a silly question and you get a silly answer." And, yet, within the proper context, the question is very sensible. An article I once read described an American Indian who, after completing an advanced degree, spent considerable time in New York City. Returning to the reservation, he wanted to impress his family with his education and sophistication. When he showed a photo of the Empire State Building to his grandfather, he was surprised to hear the question: "How many sheep will it hold?" Having never been off the reservation, the grandfather was only able to relate the photo to his own experience--rectangular buildings are for housing animals and round buildings (hogans) are for housing people.

It is easy to assume that others see the world the same way we do, but this is usually not the case. A story my stepson, Paul, once heard in an anthropology class further illustrates perceptual difference. An American was once visiting a remote tribe and was puzzled on a full-moon night to observe the most virile, handsome male tribesman doing what he perceived as a solo dance. He assumed that the young man could surely dance with his choice among available attractive females. He asked the dancer why he was dancing alone and was startled when the man responded, “I’m not dancing alone. I’m dancing with the moon.” Another fascinating illustration of cultural differences was once shared with me by William H. Eddy, Jr., a fellow faculty member at the University of Vermont. He told me of an African pygmy from the forest who was given the opportunity for the first time to travel to the open plains. He had spent all of his life in a dense forest where he became accustomed to looking at things at close range. Not long after the pygmy and his white companion emerged from the forest, some specks were observed off in the distance. The driver, turning to the pygmy, said, “Look at the buffalo.” “They can’t be buffalo,” was the reply. “They’re too small. They must be insects.” By the time the two travelers came to where the buffalo were, the pygmy was greatly agitated and wanted to leave at once. He thought a place where insects grew into buffalo had to be evil. His limited forest experience had not allowed him to perceive distant objects, and he was therefore unable to interpret his new experience as his companion had.

How do rural visitors to a city see their surroundings? How is it different from the experience of city-dwellers? How does an urbanite visiting a wilderness area perceive her surroundings? Does she have an anxiety level that affects the way she “sees”? In Yellowstone, geysers, bubbling mudpots, rising steam and hot springs are around almost every turn in the road or trail. Majestic bison routinely walk through the hot landscape, threading their way between mountain meadows and through the steaming geyser basins. In such a place, first-time visitors are excited and often jump to erroneous conclusions as they try their best to understand what is happening.

I found an example of this idea when I visited Glacier Bay, Alaska to do some training for the National Park Service. I stopped in at a visitor center and asked the ranger at the desk if he knew of any unusual circumstances at his site. And this is the story he told me:

A young man from New York City came to this park and wanted to know what he should do. I suggested that he take the self-guided nature trail out behind the visitor center. The trail was in the shape of a loop and came back to the visitor center, about a mile long over level terrain with signs explaining the flora and fauna along the way. When the man was about halfway along the loop, he could no longer see the visitor center. All he could see were mountains and trees and other unfamiliar vegetation, and he panicked. He thought to himself, "I'm lost, I don't know where to go, what to do. I'm going to die." He decided that he wanted to let his friends and family back home know what happened to him, so he took out a notepad and wrote some information for them. To make his communication complete, he took his camera out, pointed it toward his face, snapped the shutter, and thought, "Now my family can see how I looked at the last." A ranger came by after awhile to direct him, and he was ok. But the experience was not soon forgotten by us and certainly not by him.

One summer at Dunraven Pass an amusing incident occurred on the east side of the park, where some road construction was in progress. One of the road crew was a young man of college age who had decided he wouldn't shave or have his hair cut all summer. And, as long as he was going to be working outdoors, he thought he might as well get a tan. As soon as the weather was decent in June, he took his shirt off and started to turn brown. It was obvious to others that he was a very hairy individual. This was back in the day when bears were allowed to beg along the park roads. As the summer went by, he got browner and browner and looked hairier and hairier. Nothing unusual happened to him until about the first part of August when they gave him a job as flagman directing traffic at a construction site. Everything was fine until one carload of park visitors came along, took a look at him, and didn't stop at all. But as they went by, they threw him a cookie.

Chapter 4

That's One Way of Looking at It

How often do we incorrectly assume that others share our perceptions? Do we believe that our way of looking at something is the only way, or just *one* way? Is there such thing as a correct way of seeing anything? Here are a few stories to illustrate this idea.

She bade her lover a sad goodbye, climbed into her car, and began the long journey from the motel back to her summer job at the Fishing Bridge Visitor Center. The goodbye was bittersweet because her boyfriend of several years had married another woman, and she felt guilty about seeing him again.

Fifty miles or so down the road, while passing through rugged, isolated mountain terrain, she picked up a hitchhiker with a backpack. Soon the water in her car's radiator overheated, exploding into hissing steam, and they were stranded. She and her passenger searched for water and discovered a small creek several hundred yards down the mountainside. They tediously carried water up from the creek in two Sprite cans, the only containers they had. After about an hour the radiator was filled and they were on their way. When the story was told to me by the young woman, she concluded: "God gave me car trouble to punish me for doing what was wrong." "That's a possibility," I suggested, "but there's another way of looking at it. Maybe you were being rewarded somehow. Maybe the hitchhiker was there to help you in a time of need." She was flabbergasted but relieved, lightened somehow to discover there was more than one way to view her situation.

I was showing some slides one time to a group of state government employees as part of a training exercise to demonstrate how differently we all view the same event. The slides were shown without any verbal explanation and the participants were asked to write down their reactions. One slide was of a mature bull elk in prime condition along Yellowstone's Firehole River and showed off his magnificent antlers. One of the viewers wrote: "What a trophy!" This was an idea that had never occurred to me! If I were a hunter, I now saw, it would be an almost irresistible reaction. I had learned a new viewpoint, a different reaction to the same stimulus.

In the back of the Fishing Bridge Visitor Center is a sandy beach on the edge of Yellowstone Lake. The Lake is 20 miles long and behaves much like an ocean, with wind-driven waves, and foam piling up on the shore. The water's source is a glacier and is very cold. Shore birds dash after insects and youngsters run shirtless and barefoot in the warm sand. My wife and I watched a boy of about 14 run gleefully into the crashing waves, screaming and giggling as a wave engulfed him. Another boy sat at the forest edge, shivering, eyeing the powerful waves with fear. Same stimulus, same time and place, but each boy's reaction was totally different.

Chapter 5

How Natural Should a Park Be?

As I have viewed natural fires in Yellowstone, I have been grateful for the return of mineral nutrients, previously locked up in the trees, to the soil and waters of the park. I can appreciate fire because I know that heat is important to the regeneration of the lodgepole pine; that ashes washed into streams and lakes are necessary nutrients for fish and other aquatic life; that a natural fire is beneficial to certain species of birds that nest in burned snags; that a natural fire encourages renewal. The park's policy is to not fight fires. I can rejoice as I watch a natural fire, but have learned that many park visitors are unable to share my enthusiasm. For them, plumes of billowing smoke have always meant destruction and in some cases, death. It is both deeply unsettling and thrilling that something so elemental and frightening as a forest fire could be good and have its place in the order of things.

Many visitors to natural parks are repelled by the "ugliness" of nature and want to see it improved, cleaned up, prettified. In the summer of 1988 Yellowstone experienced a series of forest fires that burned tens of thousands of trees. In subsequent years, visitors would ask, "When are you going to clean up all these dead trees? They're an unsightly mess." How natural should we allow a park to be? Should rotting, odiferous, winter-killed animals be removed from areas along trails? Should we try to help elk rub the dried, bloody velvet from their antlers to improve their appearance? Should bedraggled winter hair be brushed from animals to make them look better? Let us leave things alone. Let us see nature as it is, not as we (or others) think it should be.

One day when I was working at the Old Faithful Visitor's Center, a man walked up and said, "There's an elk calf stranded on an island in the Firehole River. Someone needs to rescue it!" The mother and calf were bellowing to one another, and the calf would not follow her across. The mother waited a while and then continued on. Other park visitors also pleaded to have the calf rescued. The decision was made by the Old Faithful head ranger to leave the calf alone. As I passed by there every day afterward that summer, I looked for the calf. I never saw it again, nor did I see a carcass, that would have been visible. What should we have done? If we rescued the calf we would be violating the way of nature. Should we interfere to preserve the lives of wild creatures?

Park visitors watch thousands of gallons of steaming geyser water flow "unused" into rivers and lakes and ask, "Why don't you use that water in a swimming pool, or for cooking, or for something else worthwhile?" After all, the thermal energy is "just boiling away and going to waste" beneath the relatively thin crust of Yellowstone. It should be tapped to fuel electric-generating plants. This idea keeps surfacing every few years, most recently in West Yellowstone, just outside the park, where a private company wanted to drill to reach the pockets of energy that would be very valuable for commercial use. Thermal systems in both Iceland and New Zealand have been drilled for energy with this technology and it has depleted the natural eruptions both in strength and frequency. Is this the outcome we want?

Even if it is agreed that we want to tap this energy, the problem is: no one knows what is connected to what. One geyser might be right next to a hot spring and never show any relationship to it by its behavior. With two similar features in another location, the connection is obvious. A good example of this is Grand Geyser, whose connections with Vent and Turban Geysers are used as reliable predictors of Grand's eruptions.

Some visitors to Yellowstone are disturbed to see waterfalls generating only appreciative enthusiasm instead of kilowatts. Others are deeply troubled to see beautiful forests "allowed" to be consumed by spruce bud worms or pine bark beetles. They need help to understand that natural processes need to be left alone:

geyser waters freely, energetically depositing fresh layers of silicon dioxide on the earth's surface, the beauty of a pristine, unharnessed waterfall, the value of rotting trees in a forest.

And what about the park services provided to visitors? Should the park provide the facilities people want when on vacation? I can remember as a child visiting the swimming pool at Old Faithful. It was situated in front of the inn and was fed by the boiling waters of the nearby geysers. You could soak in this massive "hot tub" and watch geysers erupting all around you. But how did this artificially-created pool blend with or enhance the idea of nature in its pristine state? Eventually, the Park Service answered this question by eliminating the pool. Radios connect far flung"geyser gazers" and rangers so that each eruption is recorded. Elk wear collars and can be trailed in the wild. A visitor has a heart attack and another has altitude sickness. Wind-tossed pines threaten to crush a camping area if they break. What do we do? Wheelchair access, refrigeration for medications, bear spray, rental bikes, horses to ride, a federal court system for visitors at park headquarters, elk with sawed off antlers to protect visitors, licenses to carry a revolver, CD directions and commentary through your headphones, a videocam streaming Old Faithful's eruptions live on the park website…

In the early 1900s it was a popular adventure for young ladies to hike a trail leading halfway down to the bottom of the spectacular 308 foot Lower Falls of the Yellowstone River. Dressed in voluminous skirts, high-button shoes and mutton-leg sleeves, they would get to the end of the trail and, thanks to an enterprising concessioner, were offered the chance to get to the bottom of the canyon by unusual means. For a fee, a sling on a rope would lower a brave lady down to the base of the falls, a very slow and decorous version of a bungee jump. At the bottom, they would delight to stand before the spray and awesome power of the falls. Later, a series of iron steps was substituted for the rope and the trail was christened Uncle Tom's Trail after the original entrepreneur. Many travel down, and many, in all shapes and sizes, struggle back up. Are these steps appropriate in this setting? They are certainly not "natural".

It could be argued that services for people diminish nature and our experience of it. But they do allow many more people to have some kind of experience of nature, of "other". But at what cost?

Chapter 6

Don't Pick the Beer Bottles

One day, in a very different setting in South Boston, Massachusetts, I was with about fifteen experienced interpreters on a guided tour. Leading the tour were an employee of the National Park Service and a South Boston "native". The tour had not been underway long when we entered a narrow street lined by a small cemetery that had been used as a firing range for beer bottle throwers. It was a mess, but a mess with a story – a story illustrating adolescent social problems in South Boston, as the local guide explained eloquently. The "mess" had served a useful purpose: to reveal a vital fact about the area. One man asked, "When are you going to clean up all these beer bottles?" Others chimed in, "Aren't cemeteries supposed to be clean? Isn't it wrong to vandalize a sacred place like this? Littering is offensive", etc. Within moments the group went into action. Cardboard boxes materialized from somewhere and were soon filled to capacity. The industrious interpreters succeeded in transforming the littered cemetery in about fifteen minutes. While it was no longer littered with green and gold shards, it no longer told a story about neighborhood adolescents. I was the only non-participant in the cleanup, and I suppose my colleagues may have thought of me as lazy or not valuing neatness. In reality, I did not join in because I thought it wrong to alter the situation, *to superimpose my value system on a culture I was trying to understand.* Just as picking flowers from a meadow alters it, picking broken beer bottles out of a cemetery changes an historical area. Just as flowers belong in a meadow, broken beer bottles, whether we like it or not, may belong in a cemetery. If our eyes are too filled with our own values, we may be blinded to the realities that face us. Several decades ago, a small virgin forest near Burlington, Vermont, was willed to the state university. When the university treasurer went to the woods to investigate the newly-acquired property, he was appalled by all the dead wood, all the clutter, and ordered the place cleaned up immediately, before the “asset” burned to the ground. Fortunately, wiser heads prevailed, and this remnant of a time-gone-by was preserved for study.

Chapter 7

What is Your Reference?

When I trained interpreters I found that many of my experiences outside the park came in handy. Take the following example.

When my wife, Sue, turned to me and said, "It'll all be over in a week," I knew I was in deep trouble. We were at about the halfway point in our drive from our Vermont home to her childhood home in Connecticut. What was she talking about? What was going to be all over in a week? I could have said, "What is your referent? What's going to be over?" That approach, however, might have led her to assume that I hadn't been listening to her. So, to protect myself, I began replaying our conversation. We'd been talking about some people who were having marital problems. Could she mean that the friends' marriage would end in a week, or, that they'd be able to solve all their problems in a week? I continued to explore my recall of our conversation. My wife had badly strained the ligaments in her left knee just before our journey. Previously in our conversation I had asked her how the pain in her knee was. Perhaps she was saying that in a week the pain would be gone. There was yet another possibility. We were traveling in early October and the foliage was near the peak of its color. Maybe she meant the leaves would have lost their color by the time a week had passed. Bingo! She confirmed that that was it. In a week, she thought, the color would all be gone.

A little later, after our conversation had ambled along about trees, buildings, and people of her hometown – she said, "They sure have changed." Did she mean all three had changed, a combination of two had changed, or did she mean only the people of East Hartland, Connecticut? Or, perhaps her referent had nothing to do with any of these.

"Oh, look at that!" she later exclaimed, and I was perplexed as to where to look, especially since I was driving at the time. "It's so graceful!" This lack of clarity happened so frequently on our journey that "What's your reference?" became a frequent and oft hilarious exchange for both of us.

Uh, oh. My wife just poked her head into my study with the message, "Whatchamading stinks!" What's her reference? I hadn't been eating cheese, onions, or garlic. Turns out she'd stopped on the way home for Chinese takeout dinners. In her small car, the smell of the food combined with the odor of a neighbor's dog had been overwhelming. I was safe. Now I knew what she meant!

When we communicate with another person, we need to remember that s/he will attach meaning to words that may be very different from ours. Your listener may not be hearing what you intend to communicate. Here is an example.

One of the most interesting guided walks in the park is the Petrified Trees walk. Starting at 8 a.m., the assembled group is told they will be guided to a place where there are several huge upright petrified tree trunks. Because the temptation to collect specimens on this hike is strong, each time the walk is given, it follows a different route so as not to create a trail for people to use on their own. The ranger who led this hike was very experienced and had "blazed" many new trails. The distance to the trees was only two and a half miles, but it was very steep, with loose rocks and generally difficult going. It was made clear to hikers that they should wear sturdy footwear and bring a lunch to eat on the ridge among the petrified trees. One day I happened to be driving by the trailhead as a group was returning from the hike. I stopped to talk with the hikers. When I got out of my car, I noticed a highly polished limosine among the RV's, campers and travel-dusty cars in the parking lot. Standing alongside it was a uniformed chauffeur wearing leather gloves, a cap, and shiny knee-high boots. My eye was then immediately caught by a middle-aged woman coming out of the woods carrying her gleaming, red high-heeled shoes in her hands. She was dressed as if she had just been to a lively cocktail party: wide-brimmed hat askew, hair wind-tossed and disheveled, and perspiration dripped from her chin. I approached her and asked, “How was the hike?” Her reply was, “Oh, I had a terrible time! It was so steep, it was dreadful! If I had known how hard it was going to be, I would have sent my chauffeur on the hike to take pictures!” She limped to her limo, entered the opened door, and was gone.

Why did this event turn out so badly for her? She evidently had a different understanding of “steep”, “off the trail”, “difficult”, “wear sturdy shoes”, “loose rocks”, and “bring a lunch” than most people. (The other hikers shared their lunches with her). She was from a metropolitan area and the printed and spoken words of warning apparently did not register.

Chapter 8

Richness in Our Diversity

When leading nature walks in Yellowstone I learned a couple of things. One of them was that people could often contribute wonderfully to the group because of special interests and backgrounds. Also, no two groups are exactly alike. So when I gathered a group together I would start off by asking the members where they're from, what kind of work they did, how long they'd been in the park, how many walks they'd been on, etc. After we became acquainted, I explained, "I know each of you is going to be interested in different things on this walk. Some of you may be more interested in birds, or maybe the geology of the area, or buffalo, elk or marmots. Whenever you see something along the trail that interests you, I'd like you to stop me and ask about it. If you know something you'd like to share with the group, please do so." I found that this made nature walks a lot more exciting and more fun for everybody.

I had a pharmacist on a walk one day, for example, who showed a special interest in a patch of larkspur. He made the comment that pharmacists used to make a lotion from that plant for the treatment of human body lice. I asked in a joking way, "What do you mean 'used to make it' – why aren't you making it now? Wasn't it any good?" He said they didn't make it anymore because the standard of cleanliness in the United States is so high, there is no longer any problem with body lice.

This way of involving and respecting people bore fruit in staff trainings as well. In addition to taking people on nature walks, in 1967 I became supervisor of the day-to-day interpretive activities at

Old Faithful. In helping train the new staff I found it was important to recognize every person as a unique individual and encouraged them to share their special knowledge with each other. One woman was working on her master's degree in ornithology at the University of Idaho and we all learned a lot about birds from her. Another interpreter was a student of veterinary medicine and shared many insights about animals.

In leading nature walks myself and training interpreters to do so I discovered that the sharing of individual strengths and knowledge greatly benefited the group.

Chapter 9

"Say Ranger, does it ever get this hot around here?"

Nearly all of the questions asked at the visitor center desk are straightforward. "When's Old Faithful going to erupt?" "How often does it go?" "How do I find the post office?" "Do you spray for mosquitoes?" (No, they're a natural part of our environment. They are an important pollinator of some of our bog orchids and are food for some of our animals.) "How many people were killed during the 1959 earthquake?" (29, all of them just outside the Park.)

All questions are important, but once in awhile there are some memorable ones. There are hundreds, if not thousands of geysers and hot springs in Yellowstone National Park, which led one visitor to question, "How many undiscovered thermal features are there in Yellowstone?" I still don't know the answer to that one. I was temporarily without words one day when working at Yellowstone's Old Faithful Visitor Center and was asked, "Say, ranger, does it ever get this hot around here?" It was difficult not to reply with, "Of course not. What you're experiencing is only an illusion," or some similar "wise" remark. At first, I didn't clearly realize what he wanted to know, but I guessed he was inquiring if it was typical for it to be as hot as it was that day. My answer, "It's usual for it to be this hot in July at Old Faithful," seemed to satisfy him.

That same summer, at the same location, I heard a man say to someone, "Go ahead and ask him." I looked for the person he was talking to and all I could see at first were two small hands clasped to the counter and a small head of hair. Then, two big blue eyes came above the edge of the counter, and I heard a four-year-old ask, "How many baby bears does a mama bear lay every year?" While the question may have been technically inaccurate, it surely is one of the most endearing questions I've ever been asked.

"I heard that a whole family fell into Morning Glory Pool! I saw the fire truck down there and they had their hoses out. One of the crowd gathered around the pool said, 'A whole family fell into the pool and they're trying to pump them out!' Is that true?" the man asked. I responded, "No, it isn't true." I went on to explain the real story. Over the years, park visitors have been throwing rocks and all sorts of things into the pool, perhaps because they see it as a "wishing well". They're probably not malicious acts, but throwing rocks into hot springs is very harmful because any obstruction prevents the pool or geyser from behaving normally. It gets clogged up. Park administrators thought it would be a good idea to remove the debris using a novel method. We've long known that if you remove water from the top of a hot spring the loss of the weight on top will release pressure on the superheated water below and cause it to burst into steam and water. If Morning Glory's top were removed, the bottom might flash into steam and cause erupting water to flush out the rocks and debris. Theoretically it was a great idea to use the fire engine to pump the water out. The area had been roped off for visitor safety and a crowd stood just outside the rope. When the fire engine's pumps were turned on, the metal parts came into contact with near-boiling water, expanded, and seized. The plan was "scratched". The Park's main road ran by Morning Glory Pool, so people drove by, saw the fire engine and a large group of people and easily made the erroneous conclusion that "a whole family fell into Morning Glory and they are trying to pump them out!"

A huge boulder, a glacial erratic at Canyon is surrounded by trees. Said one park visitor: "Isn't it wonderful how nature put that boulder down without breaking any trees?!?"

Another summer I was leading a guided walk along the rim of the Grand Canyon of the Yellowstone River. After having looked at the magnificent sight of the Lower Falls cataracting more than 300 feet into the gorge below, a park visitor asked me, "How far would the water drop if the falls were at sea level?" At first that sounded like a dumb question, but as I tried to put myself in the place of the person who asked it, I began to make sense of it. After all, she had learned that water boils at a different temperature at sea level than at 8,000 feet, and that the plants she had been examining were affected by altitude – so, why not the falls? At least her question indicated she was alive and thinking.

One day at the Norris Geyser Basin Visitor Center, a man said, "I just saw a bear down the road with two blue ribbons fastened to its ear. What prize did it win?" I suppressed my amusement and explained why the bear was sporting ribbons. As the number of park visitors increased, conflicts between beggar bears and people became not only a nuisance but also dangerous. Park officials decided to solve the problem by forcing bears to be wild again. The garbage dumps were closed and park waste was disposed of outside the park. Bear-proof garbage cans were installed and the rule against feeding along park roads was strictly enforced. All beggar-bears were live-trapped from the roadsides and hauled away to the back country. Before releasing the bear into the wild, it was identified by attaching several ribbons. If a beribboned bear came back to the road and begged for food, it was shot. So, in answer to the man's question, no, the bear didn't win a prize but was destined for termination.

"Where is the camera?" is one of the questions most frequently asked of the staff at Old Faithful now. They are referring to the camera focused on the geyser to provide streaming video on the Park's website. It is mounted on a tall tree at the edge of the geyser area. Upon receiving an answer, a visitor will then walk in front of the camera, stand between it and the geyser and call a friend or relative on his cellphone. When the call goes through, he will wave at the camera and say, "Can you see me?" This behavior is highly annoying to me and probably distracting to others who are watching the spectacle of Old Faithful live.

One day I was in the process of interpreting the Fountain Paint Pot area for a group of park visitors. This area's chief interests are the boiling, steaming cones of red, pink, or brown miniature volcano-like structures varying in height from a few inches to several feet. There are also small ponds of bubbling mud, looking a lot like the surface of cooking oatmeal. Steam and water had, over thousands of years, worked their way through cracks and fissures of the volcanic rhyolite rock that covers much of the park and had created this mud. There are also several spectacular geysers in the area, including Clepsydra, that erupts out of several vents every few minutes. So this was the setting for one of the most memorable and unusual questions I've ever been asked during the many summers I've worked in Yellowstone. A young girl perhaps ten years old came up to me and asked, "When am I going to get to the park?" Perplexed by her question, I asked one of my own. "Do you mean Yellowstone Park?" "Yes," she replied. Her answer didn't help me understand what she wanted to know. If she had come in the nearest entrance at West Yellowstone, she had been in Yellowstone for at least 20 miles. She was standing in an area of exploding mud pots and erupting geysers. How could she not know she was in Yellowstone?

So, then I asked her, "What did you expect to find in Yellowstone Park?" She replied, "Oh, you know, green grass, swings, teeter-totters, benches, picnic tables." She was from New York City and the only park she'd had any experience with was Central Park. Her visit to Yellowstone had certainly given her a new meaning for P-A-R-K.

The meanings of words exist in the minds of the people that use them, and are not inherent in the words themselves.

Many years ago, an urban lady came to the West Yellowstone entrance of the park by train. She walked up to the entrance station and asked, "Where's the trail?" "Which trail do you mean?" I asked. She said, "The main trail. I want to walk around the park." Yellowstone is a very large park. It's 145 miles around the main scenic road inside the park. She had no idea it was that large.

I also found that some people have difficulty driving Yellowstone's roads because they're not numbered. Instead of following Highway 20 or 191, they have to learn to travel from junction to junction, just like in the old west. I remember one irate gentleman who came up to the information desk late one afternoon and demanded, "Tell me where I am!" I told him he was at Old Faithful. "Show me on the map," he said. I got the map out and pointed it out to him, and he said, "Oh my God, that's where I was this morning! I've been trying to get out of the park all day!" He had been driving around Yellowstone's scenic loop road all day looking in vain for highway numbers.

From these experiences I learned to regard all questions as worthwhile and worthy of respect. I always encourage people to ask questions, even "dumb" ones.

Chapter 10

Steamboat Geyser

Steamboat Geyser is located in the Norris Geyser Basin roughly in the center of the park. It has had an erratic eruption history since the 1800s when records began. When it does erupt, it is extremely loud and shoots about 400 feet high. It erupted about once every 7 or 9 years in the first part of the 1900s, then remained quiet for 50 years until 1961. In 1962 it erupted at least seven times and then became very active in 1963 and 1964 with 26 and 29 eruptions respectively. Since 2000, it has varied in interval from six months to eight years.

As the summer of 1962 approached, I was particularly excited to get to Yellowstone to see what was happening to Steamboat Geyser. I had heard the thermal features in the whole Norris Geyser Basin had not been this active for many decades. I also couldn't believe my good fortune to be given the position of senior seasonal interpreter there so I could share this with the increasing number of enthusiastic visitors. The volume of people suddenly visiting the site was overwhelming the staff and I helped organize and train them so that visitors could get the most out of what was happening.

My wife, four children, and I drove three-and-a-half days from Vermont to Yellowstone to begin our summer. We carried with us an electric organ, three guitars, several amplifiers, speakers as well as more mundane things like clothing and kitchen utensils. That was the summer we had an old station wagon, two car-top carriers, and a one-wheel trailer fastened to the rear bumper. The distance of 2,307 miles–I kept meticulous records--went by fairly quickly that year because we were all excited about seeing Norris.

Early the next morning, I left my exhausted family sleeping on makeshift cots and walked to the geyser basin, closely observing all the thermal activity. I particularly gave a good look at Steamboat; it was erupting every few minutes to a height of 10 to 30 feet. I had seen it do that the previous summer when I'd used my precious days off to try and catch a major eruption, but had never succeeded. Somehow this was different. After scouting the two-mile basin, full of steam, bubbling mudpots, geysers of assorted sizes, and the usual sulfur smell from this acidic area, I headed home for lunch. I told my family that they had better come back to Steamboat with me; I had a hunch that it might erupt. It was an amazingly lucky guess, since this notably fickle geyser had spurted like this many times before, but not as a preamble to a major eruption. Eating on the run, the six of us were soon huddled in a semi-circle as close to the vent as seemed 'safe'. At that time there was only a dirt trail going past the Geyser, not the wooden steps and lookout terraces that are there now. All of a sudden, the water in Steamboat's throat began to gurgle, and it began to throb upwards to thirty feet, then forty feet, and finally to over three hundred feet. It made a terrifying roar, the water flashing into steam as it rose skyward; the sound was so deafening, that we had to shout directly into one another's ear in order to be heard. Imagine standing next to a jet plane, or a huge locomotive at full speed! The ground rumbled and shook, and then small, thin rocks, about the size of dimes or quarters, began falling on us. I was wearing my broad-brimmed ranger hat, that was pelted with debris--probably small pieces of siliceous sinter broken from the geyser's plumbing. The super-heated water from the exploding geyser was rushing down the hill, washing away the broken rock and little skim of dirt that had served as a trail just minutes ago. Even 200 feet down the wash, the water was still too hot to be touched. The monster geyser still gave off hot steam and hissing before it finally retired to the hot magma many miles underground. All six of us, huddled closely together, had witnessed terror and beauty in the same instant. In that experience, which lasted about thirty minutes, the family coalesced. One of the most amazing powers of nature, exhibited in such a rare, unbelievable moment ... and we were there!

Chapter 11

Decker's Island

Mrs. Decker was a 70-year-old widow who had a passion for geysers. She was especially fond of those in the Norris Geyser Basin and loved Steamboat Geyser, which had just begun erupting fantastically high, about 300 feet, making it the world's highest geyser. Steamboat had not erupted more than 30-40 feet since 1872, when the Park was founded, so this was a major change. The intervals between eruptions varied from a few days to a few weeks and, unlike most geysers, there was no preliminary activity that warned of an eruption. One just had to sit, wait, and be lucky. Many people from the nearby campground would stand or sit all day long hoping for an eruption. One of those patient onlookers was Mrs. Decker, a spry, diminutive woman in her sixties, carrying a camera and fully covered (including hat) against the intense sun and reflection (off the white rock).

We soon began to notice that Mrs. Decker was at Steamboat every day. We enjoyed getting to know her and appreciated her determination to see a major eruption. The geyser was active all the time, splashing up to 15-20 feet every few minutes, but she was waiting for the real thing. There were three of us assigned to interpret Steamboat and nearby thermal features. We assumed she was camping at the nearby campground and walking over on the boardwalk every day. Because of the proximity of the parking area to the geyser, Mrs. Decker had begun sleeping in the back seat of her car in the parking lot. Technically she was in violation of the Park's rule that all campers use campgrounds (except backcountry campers, who had permits). Since she was using the restrooms near the parking area and she wasn't making a fire, we decided not to bother her. Plus, she was so devoted to Steamboat, and so were we.

We were perplexed about Mrs. Decker because we didn't see her close by Steamboat during the day. Where was she? Steamboat is located on a hill and at the bottom of the hill there is a stream that carries runoff from several thermal features to the Gibbon River. The stream was small, dividing into several smaller streams as it ran through a stand of lodgepole pine. Mrs. Decker had found a spot downhill from Steamboat on a space between two of these small streams where she could sit in the shade while she waited for the major eruption. The last time I saw Mrs. Decker, she was sitting on her island. From then on, geyser enthusiasts have referred to this spot as "Decker's Island".

Mrs. Decker was so devoted to Steamboat that she asked in her will for her ashes to be strewn on her island. When her family wrote to the Park asking for permission to carry out her request, permission was not granted because it is illegal to dispose of any material in the Park that is not from the Park. Years later, a Decker family member looked me up. He told me that Mrs. Decker had mentioned Ranger Bill Lewis in her correspondence and he wanted me to know that her wish had been carried out.

Chapter 12

Poor George Stories

While I was supervising the staff at Norris Geyser Basin one summer, I had a series of experiences with one of my coworkers named George that were so moving that I want to devote a chapter to it here.

George had a great enthusiasm for Yellowstone and loved to share it with people. While George and I were walking down the trail one day, we found that some vandals had jammed a log down the mouth of Vixen Geyser, and it was stuck there. George and I tried to pull the log out so the geyser could erupt again. As we were tugging away, the geyser erupted, spurting water up alongside the log, and some landed in George's shoe. The temperature of the water was several degrees above boiling and he received a very bad burn.

Since he was injured on the job, George could have taken sick leave to recover from the accident, but he was enthusiastic and so loved people and the park that he wanted to stay on the job. After treatment at the hospital, he came back to work and said, "If you'll let me work without regulation shoes and let me wear my moccasins until I get this dressing off my foot, I'll just go on working as usual." I told him, "Sure, just put your moccasins on and go to work." The next day, as George was standing in the visitor center with his moccasins on, a National Park Service official from Washington came through. He saw George with his makeshift footwear on. Without asking George why he wasn't wearing regulation shoes, the official called the chief of park interpretation, and reported him being out of uniform. An investigation was conducted and George had a lot of explaining to do.

Norris Geyser Basin is the location of the world's highest active geyser. Few of our park visitors knew anything about it. Called Steamboat Geyser, it erupts to about 300 feet, three times as high as Old Faithful. Its total eruption lasts several hours and it makes a roar so loud it can be heard a mile or two away. It's a spectacular event. George lived in the back of the museum at Norris. He had a passion for Steamboat Geyser and this was its most active summer in recorded history. He observed it a lot and shared his excitement and stories about it with visitors at campfire talks.

Since Steamboat's eruptions are unpredictable and fairly infrequent, it's difficult to catch it in play. So when it did erupt, we wanted everybody we could get hold of to see it. One morning it erupted at about 7:30, just as I was coming to work. I knew it was George's day off, but I was sure he'd want to see it, so I ran over and knocked on his door and yelled, "Steamboat's erupting!" Instead of running right over to see the geyser, George, wanting people to see it, went out to the road, stopped traffic and guided cars into the parking lot. He had dressed quickly–so quickly that he hadn't bothered to put on a necktie. Who should come along but Yellowstone's park superintendent who reported a ranger out of uniform at Norris Geyser Basin. Another investigation was conducted to discover why George was out of uniform … again.

I received a third call from park headquarters about George. This time it was a complaint that George was telling "dirty stories" at his evening campfire program. That didn't sound like George to me, so I told him about the complaint and we were both perplexed. We talked about all the possibilities we could think of and finally came up with a likely one.

The Norris Geyser Basin campground is only about two miles from Steamboat Geyser. Campers there can easily hear the eruption, especially at night when there is almost no traffic noise. One night at about 10:00 p.m. Steamboat began to violently erupt. There was a full moon that bore a silvery moonbow made from the spray and steam of the eruption. Rainbows from the sunlight are fairly common, but a moonbow is exceptionally rare and beautiful. Most of the campers had been hanging around the geyser all day, waiting, hoping for a major eruption. When the campers heard the roar, they knew what was happening and made haste to their vehicles. As it was bedtime, some brought their sleeping bags or blankets. Not wanting to miss a minute of Steamboat's eruption, most of them came dressed (or undressed) as they were, in pajamas and nightgowns. Soon the hillside was covered with about 50 campers carrying their kerosene lanterns or flashlights, all of which seemed unnecessary as there was so much moonlight. The eruption was very loud and water exploded in every direction, unpredictably, drenching people with steam and spray. George and I both witnessed this unusual, exciting, and memorable event. Even 40 years later, it is almost too impressive to describe.

A year or so later, George was telling this story at a campfire talk and concluded with something like, "It was a beautiful sight. The most powerful geyser in the world was erupting. There was a moonbow in the spray, a full moon, and a crowd of campers in their pajamas or nighties wrapped in blankets, all carrying lights of some sort. It was hard to know where to look." This story is the only one George and I could think of that could be remotely labeled a "dirty story". I reported my findings to park headquarters and there was no reply. Perhaps they were satisfied with my explanation because I had no more complaints about George. He continued at Yellowstone for several more exemplary seasons. When I last heard, he was working for the Montana Fish and Game Department. Probably the dress code was much more casual!

Chapter 13

Out of Uniform Experiences

On the road between Mammoth Hot Springs and the Norris Geyser Basin there are two small bodies of water identified by a sign as the "Twin Lakes". These lakes owe their existence to runoff from hot springs and perhaps a spring or two at their bottoms. The resultant water is fairly acidic and warm. As I drove by these "lakes" one day, I saw a park visitor trying his luck at catching a fish. I saw him cast a couple of times. I thought I should tell him there couldn't be any fish in the South Twin Lake. So, I pulled my car over to the side of the road behind his and explained that I was a park ranger out of uniform on my way to work, that there weren't any fish in the lake, and explained why. He looked me over and said, "I know you rangers. You're always trying to keep the best fishing places for yourselves." That said, he turned his back to me and resumed casting.

Parents are often an embarrassment to their children. My daughter recalls a time when she was about 14 years old, when the family was traveling along Yellowstone's main road and we spotted a man emerging from the forest carrying a large set of elk antlers. Male elk shed their antlers annually so as to grow new ones. Usually the antlers get larger as the animal ages–until in old age there is less antler growth. So, shed antlers are often seen by park visitors. It's unlawful to do more than observe them in their natural habitat; collecting naturally-occurring specimens of all kinds is prohibited. So there we were observing the law being broken, and I was out of uniform and not allowed to make an arrest. I decided to explain to the park visitor that it's unlawful to do what he's doing, that he can't take antlers with him, that he has to leave them. He told me he didn't have to pay attention to me because I was out-of-uniform and that he could get away with it. So, I informed him that I would follow him to his car, make note of his license plate and report him to the nearest ranger station. Meanwhile back at the car, my daughter was, as she now tells me, highly embarrassed by my behavior.

Dr. Sam Beal, Yellowstone's historian during most of the time I was working there, told me of a place in the Park where there were a couple of wickiups used by the Shoshone Indians before Yellowstone was designated as the first national park. Wickiups are structures shaped like teepees but composed entirely of slender lodgepole pines. Still standing after more than 100 years, they were a sight to behold. The sagging structures were off trail and were known to exist by only a handful of people. Two of my sons, two of their friends, and I bushwhacked to them and appreciated seeing specimens of another time. We arrived back at the Specimen Creek Trail in the northwest section of the Park and shortly encountered a father and his two sons. They were carrying buckets and bags full of petrified wood and other geological treasures. After seeing the wickiups unaltered by collectors, it was especially upsetting to see these things collected in buckets and bags. I explained to them that specimen collecting in the Park was illegal, that the Park's treasures were there for future generations to enjoy. At this point, one of the man's sons said, "But what if we're collecting specimens to sell in our rock shop?" The father hastened to quell any further outbursts from the boy. It's one thing, I thought, to collect for one's private enjoyment, but worse to rob the Park for money. I was out-of-uniform, unable to make an arrest. I told them I was a park ranger, that I was going to report their illegal behavior, and that they would have to return the specimens to where they'd found them. They agreed to do this and we went on our way. But, we didn't trust them and circled back to the part of the trail they'd have to use to return to their vehicle. We never saw them again, but when we reached the spot where we'd first encountered them, we found the buckets and bags full of specimens left in the middle of the trail. They had apparently dropped their load and gone off-trail when they heard us, planning to return later. The five of us had the joy of returning the specimens to the wilderness, and as we hurled them we shouted with glee, hoping that future generations would enjoy them (but leave them there!)

Chapter 14

Harmonious Diversity

One summer I was asked to do some training at Carlsbad Cavern National Park, New Mexico. One morning before work I stood alone at the entrance to the caverns watching thousands of bats returning. The night before I had been part of a large crowd of about 1,000 observing this phenomenon and had found the experience disappointing. The sounds of shuffling feet, shrieks of delight and muffled conversations had masked the amazing flight sounds. When I expressed my feeling to Frank Walker, the park's chief of interpretation, he suggested that I come back the next morning at about 5:00 to observe the bats return. I followed his advice and had one of the most moving experiences of my life. As I approached the cavern opening, the sounds were overwhelming. They were not the high-pitched squeaks I might have expected, but the sounds of ripping bed sheets. Imagine about 100 people gathered in a group ripping pieces of bed sheets in random sequence. I later learned that the sounds were made by the bats folding their wings as they flew into the cavern. Place these sounds, that were audible at several hundred feet, in the cool air and sharp light of dawn. Visualize great numbers of black plum-sized pellets hurtling past you to merge with the darkness of the cavern's mouth. You are all alone and aware only of your own breathing and pulsing blood. After about 30 minutes of watching in awe, the sun's rim gently floods this mountain ruggedness and swallows begin to leave the cavern in search of food. The swallows and bats pass each other in synchronous harmony. Sunlight increases and the opening of the cavern is slowly visible, transformed, until, like an exposed Polaroid film, a peacefully-grazing mule deer materializes just over the cavern entrance. As I have relived this experience, I have become aware of the diversity that was involved. The bats, by themselves, *or* the swallows, *or* the deer would have been impressive, but I believe it was the combination, all in apparent harmony, that elevated the experience to a very special place in my memory.

Chapter 15

Pocket Basin Stories

In Yellowstone's Lower Geyser Basin about eight miles north of Old Faithful there's a trail-less area called the Pocket Basin. It is along the Firehole River and home to a large number of mudpots of various sizes and colors. Mudpots are hot springs with very little water, a lot of clay minerals and decomposed rhyolite. Rhyolite is a volcanic rock that over geologic time has been altered by acids, heat, water and steam. Imagine a pot of boiling oatmeal 15 feet across and five feet deep and that will give you an idea of how the mudpots look and sound. The 1959 earthquake made more heat available to these mudpots, causing increased activity. Mud sometimes exploded onto the nearby vegetation. I began giving interpretive walks in the area. As we'd walk through the forest on our way to the mudpots, I'd tell my group, "As we walk through the trees to the mudpots, I want you to be aware of an odor that's new to the area. When you smell something unusual, let me know." Someone would smell sulfur and I'd say, "Yes, that's sulfur in the air, but that's not new." "It smells like something's burning." "You're close," I'd answer. Someone else would often say, "It's sort of sweet." "Yes," I'd respond. "What does it make you think of, especially if you're from Maine, New Hampshire, or Vermont?" "Oh," someone would say, "it smells like sap being boiled to make syrup." "That's it!" Then we'd talk about how the '59 earthquake released steam through the cracks in the earth and had actually cooked the roots of the trees surrounding us! And was still doing so. The sweet carbohydrates in the root system smelled like burning maple syrup as they heated.

On the way to the Pocket Basin one passes the Ojo Caliente Hot Spring. It's a roiling, boiling spring with a deep blue color. A park visitor once told me of an observation he made there. A small group of bison was on the road by Ojo Caliente when the animals shifted toward the pool and one of them was pushed into the super-heated pool and quickly died. Not long thereafter, the odor of cooked bison attracted a bear that walked back and forth at the side of the spring, trying to figure out how to retrieve the boiled bison floating on top of the water that smelled so appetizing. The bear went to the edge of the pool and reached out to grab the prize, burned his or her paw, and retreated to some nearby sand and rubbed its paw into it, apparently trying to cool it. The bear tried to reach the bison several times before giving up and walking away. Later in the day I drove to Ojo Caliente to see what was happening, but the floating, thoroughly-cooked bison was gone. Either the wind had blown the bison near to the pool's edge and another bear (or others) had enjoyed a feast, or perhaps it had sunk to the bottom of the spring. Bones are often found in spring bottoms. In fact, one of Yellowstone's features is called Skeleton Pool.

Years later, when I was training others to give the Pocket Basin guided walk, I had an experience I shall long remember. The leader of the walk was a geologist by background and I was along to observe. He picked up a rock and began telling how it came to be there, what minerals it contained and so forth, when an insect crawled out from under the rock he was holding. Someone asked, "What insect is that?" Fortunately, he knew and gave some interesting information about it. Then he threw the rock back on the ground and someone in his group said, "Would you mind putting that insect's home back where you found it?" It was a good reminder that one needs to value of all forms of life.

Chapter 16

"Oh, you poor dear!"

I lived in a cabin one summer at Old Faithful that was heated by a wood stove. One day I was chopping wood for the stove when the ax handle broke. I had much difficulty in the insertion of the new handle. I shaved quite a bit of wood off the top of the handle but I didn't have the right tools and made slow progress. Finally, in exasperation, I placed the handle across the chopping block, stepped up on the block and stood on the handle to hold it in place while I tried to hammer the metal head onto the wood. Yes, it was a dumb thing to do, as I soon discovered. The chopping block toppled and I found myself on the ground. I had come down hard on my left elbow and my arm wasn't feeling too good.

The pain compelled me to drive to park headquarters at Mammoth Hot Springs (about 50 miles away) where I presented myself to the doctor at the infirmary. He determined by x-ray that I had chipped a piece of bone off the tip of my elbow and that the tendon was still attached to the bone chip. He thought that the chip would be pulled back into place if we could straighten the arm so this "natural healing" could take place. He found two pieces of plywood about two feet by two inches and sandwiched my arm between them, wrapping the boards into place with an extensive piece of ace bandaging. With my stiff-board arm, I returned to Old Faithful. And then what? I was eligible for sick leave but decided with a few adjustments I could still function as an interpretive park ranger. There wasn't any way I could put my "boarded" arm through my uniform shirt so I cut the sleeve out of the shirt, put my bandaged arm through the hole and went back to work.

While walking through the geyser basins talking with park visitors, you can imagine my appearance led to a lot of "What happened to you?" type of questions. Some people wanted to know if I didn't know better than to feed the bears. Had I been splashed by an erupting geyser? "Don't you know better than to get too close to the thermal features?" After several days of this good-natured bantering, I became irritable and regret to say that when a sweet "little, old lady" asked what had happened to my arm, I responded with, "I put my arm inside a geyser to turn it on and didn't pull it out fast enough." She looked at me with genuine concern and tears began to well up in her eyes. She patted me on the shoulder and said, "Oh, you poor, poor dear." I knew immediately that I had seriously erred. I wanted to take the words back, but I could no more do that than push Old Faithful back down its orifice. I learned from that experience not to take lightly any question that's asked of me.

Later, another x-ray showed the bone chip hadn't moved at all. Fortunately, I had a cousin who was a surgeon at a hospital at Rexburg, Idaho and he removed it and gave it to me as a souvenir of my "learning experience".

Chapter 17

Six Lemonade Hike

On a hot summer day, a fellow ranger and I decided to explore the bottom of the Yellowstone River Canyon several miles downstream from the famous Lower Falls. We wanted to see the canyon from a different perspective, wilder and away from people. We walked several miles along the rim of the canyon and then headed down a ravine on an unmarked "trail". We'd been told about this access to the canyon's bottom and were eager to explore. We had to carefully watch every step, holding on to trees and bushes to slow our descent. The footing was a loose and crumbly powdered rhyolite. Eons ago, this immense canyon had been a geyser basin. The overlying rock had been altered by hot water, steam and acidic hydrogen sulfide gases passing through it under pressure. All this thermal activity made the rock soft and crumbly and it was easily washed away by the torrents of the Yellowstone River over centuries of time. As we hiked we saw that the river had eroded the rock, revealing a fantastic, multi-hued spectacle, the primary colors being yellow mixed with purple, red, brown and green. After an hour or two we were at the river experiencing its beauty and the power of its spray. It was overwhelming and refreshing, but it made us thirsty. We hadn't brought any water in our backpacks because we knew the river water was pure enough to drink. We would drink our fill when we got to the bottom of the canyon and, just before leaving, we'd drink again for the return trip. We thought that would be enough.

We had brought our fishing poles and soon discovered that every cast resulted in responses from the native trout. We wanted to continue fishing but we had also planned to explore the canyon. How could we keep the fish fresh while we explored? We came up with the idea of building a small pool along the river's edge with water running in and out of it. We put the lifeless fish in "our" pond and proceeded to explore. We found green plant life growing at steamy seeps, small mud pots, and colors of every hue. Our exertion had tired us and we decided to pick up our fish and head for the rim. When we returned to our pond, it was empty. One of the sights we'd enjoyed as we explored were osprey flying high above the river, hunting for fish. Also known as fish hawks, no doubt they had spied our fish pond and helped themselves. But there was no evidence; the fish were just gone. Oh well, we'd been guilty of violating one of the Park rules: "Don't feed the wildlife". The afternoon had become hot and dry as we tried to find the unmarked "trail" we had used for our descent into the canyon. We hadn't marked it on the way down to preserve the primitive character of the place. Yet, we should have marked it in some temporary way that we could remove later. A big mistake. We finally found what we thought was the place, took our last drink from the river and began our climb. It was much more difficult going up, of course. We had slid down the loose, broken rock fairly easily, but to find something to hang on to going up was challenging. We did a lot of hand-over-hand grasping while our feet were sliding back about half the distance. We were hot and dripping with sweat. When we finally we made it to the top of the canyon we turned to look ahead and saw another canyon between us and the "real rim". In reality we had climbed to the top of an "island" out in the canyon. Our thirst and fatigue were intense, but we had no choice. We had to go all the way down into the canyon again and back up to the canyon rim. Oh, the thirst! I still remember how woozy I was. Unfortunately, this descent had no promise of a river at the bottom to slake our thirst.

When we finally made it to the "real" canyon rim, I turned to my companion, and said, "I'm thirsty!" Perhaps I can help you know my meaning for "thirsty" by telling you what happened next. We drove to the soda fountain at the Canyon Village and we each ordered two tall lemonades. And, when they were gone, we each ordered two more and we were finally assuaged by two more. For me, that day, thirsty meant six tall glasses of lemonade at one sitting.

On another occasion years before, the word "thirsty" had an entirely different meaning, and was actually quite important in my life. It was 1942, Pearl Harbor had been bombed and I had applied for the U.S. Navy's V-12 program. I was in the process of undergoing a physical examination by the Navy to see if I would qualify. I stepped on the scale and was one pound short of the minimum, 120 pounds. The Navy chief conducting the exam frowned, shook his head, and then brightened, and said, "Are you thirsty?" I didn't immediately catch his meaning. When he added, "There's plenty of water in the room next door", and looked straight at me, I suddenly became "thirsty". I asked to be excused, went next door and drank as much water as I could hold. When I went back to the examining room, I tipped the scales at 120 pounds. The Navy V-12 program led to many adventures as an officer aboard an aircraft carrier, primarily in the Pacific, but that's another story.

Chapter 18

"When is Old Faithful going to erupt?"

Over the years I have been greatly impressed with the variety of perceptions people bring to Yellowstone. Most visitors come expecting to see two things–bears and the Old Faithful geyser. They have heard that Old Faithful erupts regularly and some believe that it erupts every hour on the hour and that you can set your watch by it. Actually, since 1870 the eruptions have averaged about 65 minutes apart, varying between 33 minutes and 98 minutes. So these roughly one million eruptions over 140 years have varied 50 percent from the average in the time between eruptions. Nonetheless, people arrive every day in the park with the expectation that it is regular, and we had problems as a result.

Though Old Faithful's eruption isn't precisely regular, it is predictable. You simply need to know when it played last and how long it played. (In the park we refer to geysers as erupting or "playing".) The interval between eruptions is longer if the previous eruption played for a long time. Sometimes I would come in from the woods after taking a group on a nature walk of a couple of hours and someone would come running up to me and ask, "What time is Old Faithful going to erupt?" When I would say I don't know, the park visitor probably wondered what was the matter with me. Every ranger in Yellowstone should know when Old Faithful is going to play!

One evening in 1959, just before midnight, Yellowstone experienced a powerful earthquake, 7.5 on the Richter scale. Its center was 25 miles away at Hebgen Lake. There were some people sitting out near Old Faithful that evening a little after ten o'clock.

Old Faithful is different at night. There aren't many people around, it's quiet and peaceful, and you can hear the water splash as it comes cascading down. Because the nights are usually quite cool in Yellowstone even in the middle of the summer, the steam rises for a long time and the geyser appears to play longer. It can be magical out there late at night.

As visitors often do, the people observing that night got the idea that "Old Faithful is different tonight. Something's going on!" And then the earthquake happened! One of these people was a newspaper reporter for the *Salt Lake Tribune* in Salt Lake City, Utah. He wrote a long article about how Old Faithful gave warning of the earthquake because it played and played just before the quake. The '59 earthquake did affect the subsequent activity of almost 100 percent of the geysers in Yellowstone, greatly increasing some and decreasing others. There is no evidence that Old Faithful acted differently just before the quake, however.

Chapter 19

Learning from Negatives

I've learned a lot about communication by observing interpreters in action. Here are three examples of negative experiences I've had that taught me a great deal.

Many interpreters, having found what "works" on a walk, keep on using the same old approach. One summer a few years ago, a new hot spring broke out at Mammoth Hot Springs. While it was of relatively minor interest during its first summer, by the second summer it had developed into one of the park's most spectacular sights. The new spring was off the regular trail and could be seen only on a conducted walk. I was auditing a walk in the vicinity and reveled in the joy I knew the group would experience when they saw it. To my amazement, the interpreter took great pains to bypass the new feature as she talked about everything else. After the walk, when I asked her why she didn't take the group to the new feature, she replied, "The spring wasn't there last summer when I first gave this walk, and, since it was new, I didn't know what to say about it. I was afraid of giving the wrong information." It was the end of July. She had been bypassing this splendid opportunity for two months because she was afraid to give the walk differently from the year before.

On another occasion, our guided walk began in an open mountain valley. The interpreter started by giving us his last name only, very stiffly and formally. Then he asked the group whether they'd like to hear about the Indians who once inhabited the area or about the geology of the area. The group voted overwhelmingly in favor of the Indians. My pleasure in the interpreter's involving the group in the process of agenda-setting was short-lived, as he announced, “It’s important for you to know about the geology, so I’ll tell you about that first, then the Indians.” After twenty minutes or so of presenting a disorganized mélange of technical geological jargon, he told us two unrelated, confusing Indian legends. Finally, after thirty minutes of being at the same place, he moved the group to a dripping rock wall. “There are some interesting organisms living on this rock wall,” we were told, “and if I’d remembered to bring the hand lenses, you could see them.” After limping through a futile verbal description of what we were missing visually, we moved to another site where we learned that, “This is where they were making a movie and the bare-breasted Indian maiden went scrambling over the rock.” Nothing else, just that. Later on, unable to identify a flower, the interpreter said, “If I’d walked the trail in preparation for this walk, I’d have seen that flower and would have looked it up, but this my first walk this season.”

A third example of learning from a negative experience occurred during an event that was advertised as a weather walk. Park visitors were advised to meet in the visitor center lobby. At the time, I was doing a nationwide study for the National Park Service on the interpretation of energy. I was attracted to the walk because I saw it as appropriate for the interpretation of solar and wind energy. Three other park visitors and I were patiently waiting in the lobby even though it was five minutes past the scheduled time for the walk. All of a sudden a loud screeching voice from at least fifty feet away, on the opposite side of the lobby, said something like, “If you’re going on the weather walk, come on.” The words were so indistinctly articulated, I’ve never been positive exactly what she said. The other visitors and I looked at each other inquisitively, non-verbally asking if that had been an announcement of the walk. By now, we had located the source of the voice, just in time to see her slip out a side door. The four of us scampered across the lobby and through the door just in time to see our “leader” across the courtyard. Having been “caught”, the interpreter stood tapping her foot as she awaited the arrival of her breathless charges. “We’re going to the weather box,” she said, “where I’m going to take the day's weather." She whirled in the crushed rocks of the pathway and in no time we had covered the 100 feet to the grilled box that housed thermometers and other devices. Lifting the door to the wooden structure, she announced, "I'm now recording today's maximum temperature which is 87." Having written that down, she said, "And now I'm recording last night's minimum temperature which was 65." Then, cranking the handle of a fan, she explained, "I'm determining the relative humidity." She then checked the precipitation gauge and announced it was dry. "Any questions?," she queried. Desperately anxious for dialogue, I asked how today's readings compared with other readings for this time of year. "Oh, they're always just about the same," she asserted and followed her meaty reply with, "That's all," and stomped off with her data. I was flabbergasted.

You probably figured out where the communication went astray in these three stories. If you want to know more about the learning principles demonstrated in them, see Appendix B.

Chapter 20

Sweet *and* Skunky

If you were asked to describe the odor of the sky pilot flower (Poleminimum viscosum), assuming you were familiar with this plant, what would you say? Until very recently I would have unhesitatingly described the scent as skunky. It turns out that I would have been only half right. According to Candace Galen ("The Smell of Success," *Natural History*, July, 1985, pp. 29-35), while the common perception is that the sky pilot *always* has a skunky odor, in reality some smell sweet while others smell *both* sweet *and* skunky. This may seem trivial but it says something about human behavior. She supposes that the misperception that all sky pilots smell skunky comes from the fact that the skunky smelling plants only grow at timberline (lower elevation), while the sweet smelling variety is found in the tundra at higher elevation. "Thus," she writes, "hikers are likely to encounter the unpleasant morph first, and since the two varieties look identical, they probably avoid smelling sky pilot higher up on the trail." If Galen's explanation is correct (which seems reasonable), it contains some important implications. How often do we make assumptions based on inadequate data that turn out to be false? For example, if you have little experience with children and have a brief encounter with some unruly ones, do you assume that all children are unruly? If you are an interpreter giving nature walks, if you lead a dull group of adults who don't seem to want to participate, do you conclude that all adults don't want to be involved? In our example of the sky pilot flower, will you decide not to smell the flower at higher elevation because you want to avoid the bad smell?

Every day we collect experiences to aid in navigating future ones. We need to be constantly on guard, however, against the disease known as “hardening of the categories.” We should be cognizant of what *is* rather than what *was* at one time. When teaching students in a classroom or park visitors, one often finds a good way to present a lecture or interpret a lighthouse. This runs the risk of becoming *the way* to do it. Once *the way* has been discovered, there is no need for examining other ways of giving the light house significance. Safe in the comfort of knowing one has “arrived,” one can keep on doing the same thing *ad infinitum*.

Chapter 21

Sacagawea and Me

When the Lewis and Clark party approached the Great Falls of the Missouri River, the Indian woman Sacagawea became seriously ill. According to Meriwether Lewis' journal, it wasn't clear to them if she would survive. She was an extremely valued member of the group for her knowledge of the territory, ability to smooth relations with the Indians they met and her use of plants as food and medicine. What should they do? What medication should they give her? One member of the Corps had an idea. As he'd been exploring the area he found a spring across the river from the encampment and it was giving off sulfurous odors. Maybe that would be helpful. He rowed across the river and filled a wooden cask from the sulfurous spring. Sacagawea drank the water and quickly recovered. At least one historian has surmised that it was the amount of water that revived her because she was dehydrated, not the sulphur content. Nevertheless, the water revived her.

As an avid reader of the Lewis and Clark journals, I was intrigued by this incident and tried several times to find the spring from which Sacagawea had drunk. When the National Park Service decided to build a visitor center near the Great Falls, I was invited to come help train the staff. I agreed to do it if they would show me Sacagawea's spring. They said they didn't know where it was but knew a man who did, so the arrangement was made for him to lead us. I invited my wife Sue and two of my favorite Yellowstone hiking companions, Riley and Pat McClelland. The five of us hiked out about three miles on an unmarked trail and there it was : circular, with a diameter of about 10 feet, overflowing copiously, deep blue in color and encircled by a rich growth of yellow monkey flowers.

I wanted to drink some water from the same spring that Sacagawea had but the guide said he would not recommend it. "Why not?" I said with deep disappointment. "Because the ducks and geese swim in it, and when hunting season comes, a lot of buckshot winds up in the bottom of the spring. You might get lead poisoning." Taking a chance, I scooped up a handful and communed with Sacagawea over the degradation of an historic site.

Chapter 22

Lost at Lonesome Mountain

My daughter Kathy was only two years old when my wife and I began living in Yellowstone during the summer. As a child, she often went hiking with me and learned to love the flowers, the animals, and the thermal features. Over the years, she and her brothers took turns helping me with my evening interpretive programs by operating the slide projector. In those days it was a push-pull, take-the-old-slide-out/put-in a-new-one, primitive operation. The children also operated the lights and the audio system. As a teenager, Kathy began to work for the concessionaires who operated the stores, lodging, and restaurants. She was employed for several summers selling souvenirs and waitressing at various eateries from soda fountains to fine dining rooms. Graduating from college with a degree in speech pathology, she moved to California to practice her profession. She later married Scott, a fellow Yellowstone summer employee, and now they were coming back to Yellowstone to relive her childhood years with a brief visit.

"What's the best way to celebrate this occasion?" I asked myself. She'd already been to nearly every spot in Yellowstone. Then I thought of Lonesome Mountain. Located just outside Yellowstone's northeast entrance, the mountain rises to 11,409 feet and looks like the top of a vanilla ice cream cone that's a little flattened at the top and decorated by greenish stripes. The dome shape is volcanic in origin and the green stripes are cracks and crevices in the rock filled with the growth of trees and bushes. There is a stunning view of it across Beartooth Lake from a pullout on the

Beartooth Highway (U.S. 212). I decided it would be a good spot to bring Kathy and a small group for lunch.

Attending the picnic were my wife Bobbie Jean, Kathy, her husband Scott, my three sons Britt, Jim and Roger, one of their friends and a friend of Kathy's. Altogether there were nine of us drinking in the beauty of Lonesome Mountain as seen across Beartooth Lake. Inspired by the the view, someone voiced what all of us were thinking, "Let's climb that mountain!" It looked so close, maybe three miles away, and we were all in good physical shape and experienced hikers.

We should have known not to do this hike without better preparation. We had no topographic map, no compass, and there was no marked trail. However, the mountain was always in view so finding it was easy. The climb to the top was difficult but the view from the summit was breathtakingly beautiful. We figured the distance was closer to eight miles instead of three. We had the place all to ourselves and we were full of joy. One of our group was so exhilarated, he tore his Vietnam draft card into tiny pieces exclaiming, "Hell no, I won't go!" Not all of us made it to the top. Scott had decided, after about two hours of walking, that he couldn't make it without his cigarettes, left in the car, and he turned back. Upon reaching his locked car he realized that Kathy had the keys so he couldn't get in to get his cigarettes. (He did finally assuage his need by begging a smoke from a sympathetic driver).

Meanwhile, back at the summit, the remaining eight of us began our plans to return to the parking area. We spotted Beartooth Lake and aimed ourselves in that direction. The trouble was that our view of the lake was often obscured by trees, ravines, and other rocks. We hadn't planned our return before we set out. There were abundant trails, but they were game trails going off in a variety of directions. We quickly realized that we should have paid more attention to landmarks to guide us back. Walking toward a towering mountain is simple; descending while looking for a lake is tough. We tried following streams that may have been on their way to Beartooth Lake, but this didn't seem to work either. We were becoming quietly exhausted. Daylight faded, and as night fell,

Gary's vision diminished significantly–he had brought only his prescription sunglasses! We realized we were lost and this realization fell hardest on me. I thought, "Here I am, father of four of the hikers, husband to one, senior to everyone in the group … and with so many summers as a park ranger."

As we sat to ponder our dilemma, a full moon began to rise, illuminating our surroundings and giving us an idea of which way was north. I had also noticed the night before in which quadrant of the sky the moon rose. We picked a direction and headed off. Before long the moon brightened the landscape enough for us to recognize places we'd passed on our way up. With a mixture of relief and exhilaration, we found the cars. It was now 11:00 p.m. and there was Scott, waiting alone in the dark by the car. Moral: Before beginning a trip, plan its ending.

Chapter 23

Shake, Rattle, and Roll

Kathy Lewis Scerra, my daughter

August 17, 1959--11:37 p.m. It was a cool, dark, peaceful evening, like most summer nights in Yellowstone. At our elevation of 7,300 feet, the sky was sprinkled with countless stars, and the scent of the pines that surrounded the Old Faithful employee housing area permeated the air. My father, a seasonal park ranger naturalist, my mother, my three younger brothers, and I were sound asleep in our tiny, one-bedroom apartment. The oldest of four children, I had turned twelve that summer, and my brothers were eight, five, and four months old. We were exhausted after a day of entertaining relatives who were visiting from Florida. They had especially enjoyed exploring the sand dunes near St. Anthony, Idaho, and Big Springs, origin of the Henry's Fork branch of the Snake River. That night, my great-grandmother, great-aunt and uncle, and two cousins were sleeping a couple of miles down the road at the Old Faithful Inn cabins. Although they weren't impressed by our family's humble summer housing, they didn't know what we knew--that our place was considered an upgrade from previous summer residences that didn't include indoor plumbing! Our apartment was the end unit of three in a long, one-story wooden building.

Suddenly, the evening's peace was shattered. The family was awakened by the building shaking and my father shouting to my mother, "I've got Roger, you get Jim!" He grabbed my baby brother out of the crib and my mother groggily responded, "What's the matter?" My dad exclaimed, "It's an earthquake!" "Are you sure?"

she muttered. Then I asked, “How do you know?”, and he said what all parents say, “I just know!” My eight-year-old brother, Britt, and I ran outside with our dad, but my mom stayed indoors, fearing that a cataclysmic fissure might open up and swallow her, like she’d seen in the movies. I believe my five-year-old brother slept through the whole thing! The actual quake lasted thirty to forty seconds, but it seemed much longer.

By now, many other residents were gathering outside, excitedly trying to determine what had happened and what might happen next. No one knew if this had been a local event or more widespread. In our remote location, there was no TV to turn on, no local radio to tune in, and no phone service. My father wanted to drive down to the ranger station, but my mother insisted he not leave her alone with the kids. After a while, a ranger patrol car came down to check on us and assess any damage. He told us that the earthquake had been a major one and had been felt over a large area. It was not until the next morning that we learned the 7.5 Richter scale earthquake had its epicenter near Hebgen Lake, Montana, about 35 miles from Old Faithful, and had been felt as far away as Washington state! We also discovered, sadly, that 28 people in the Madison River Canyon lost their lives that night, when half of a 7,600 foot mountain slid down over their campground and buried the sleeping campers. People and cars were tossed into the air by the strong winds generated by the landslide.

Slowly, in our neighborhood, everyone returned to their homes. No one had been hurt and there wasn’t any substantial damage to our apartment. A mirror had fallen, but not broken, and books had been knocked from their shelves. Some furniture had slid into new places, but all of this was minor. After we all climbed back into our beds, tremors of varying strength continued to shake the house all night long. They came in long, rolling waves, and we could feel them moving down from the other end of the building and then under us. Each time a new wave began, my brother would announce, “Here comes another one!” Needless to say, we didn’t get much sleep that night.

My relatives also had quite an exciting experience down in the tourist cabin area. They were sleeping soundly when they were awakened by the earthquake that "'bout knocked the tar out of us!" They wondered if the largest, most powerful, and very unpredictable Steamboat Geyser might be erupting and causing the ground to shake! Many of the visitors in the other cabins were frantically grabbing their things and trying to drive away, an extremely unwise decision under these conditions. The next day, my great-grandmother told us the event had been "so terrible", but my mother answered, "What's so bad? Nobody's hurt and you'll remember this for years!" That was for sure.

The next morning, while my father was at the ranger station getting the latest news, my mother put my baby brother into a plastic tub for his bath on the kitchen table. Next to the table in the tiny efficiency kitchen was a water heater, on top of which leaned a metal tray that covered the stove when it wasn't being used. All of sudden, my mother felt the beginning of another strong aftershock (6.3), and just as she grabbed my brother out of the tub, the heavy metal tray slipped off the water heater and crashed down into the tub! My brother credits our mom with saving his life!

We all spent the rest of the day in the geyser basins, observing the exciting, major changes in thermal activity. The park roads between Old Faithful and West Yellowstone had been closed due to rockslides and dangerous conditions, but who could resist driving to Lower Geyser Basin to watch Clepsydra Geyser erupt from all four vents simultaneously and constantly, something that had never been seen before! We had it all to ourselves. Spotted by a government official who was assessing the situation from a plane flying overhead, we were later reported to the rangers for being there!

As an adult, I've experienced several major quakes in both California and New York, but none of them compares with the Yellowstone earthquake of 1959!

An addendum to the story by Bill Lewis

While the Lewis family was shaken out of bed by the '59 quake, a fellow park ranger was parked with his love interest in the Fountain Paint Pots area eight miles north in the Lower Geyser

Basin. The couple was impressed with the beauty of the rising steam and the sound of burbling mud nearby. All of a sudden their car began to shake violently. Startled, they began to figure out what was happening. "Maybe there's a bear under us trying to tip us over," she said. "I'll check it out," he replied, as he opened the car's door and stepped out. He'd majored in geology as a student, and now realized he was experiencing a first-class geological happening. "It's an earthquake!" he shouted. She joined him outside the car and as they gazed out over the Lower Geyser Basin they witnessed the sight of all of the geysers and the usually quiescent pools (about a dozen) simultaneously erupting wildly. The nearby mud pots were explosively throwing mud in every direction, more than they'd ever seen. The earthquake had opened new fissures in the earth's crust and was releasing a tremendous amount of thermal energy!

By the way, the two of them lived happily ever after.

Chapter 24

Hypothermia at Pine Creek Lake

Suzanne Kusserow, my wife

Bill and I met after raising our families, but before any relationship could develop, I had to be tested for permanent compatibility, which meant: Could I love Yellowstone as much as he did?

I had been to Yellowstone before. As a young girl I had traveled there with my father, a professor of botany who had done his PhD field work in Oregon and Washington and had hiked and camped over much of the western states. Therefore, this current introduction to these activities was not new to me. My growing-up years were in the northwest corner of Connecticut, which was still rural and we lived in a log house in the middle of a state forest. I have since spent most of my adult years in northern Vermont. So I didn't think I needed more orientation to rural settings.

My first adult visit to the Park was with Bill and my three children, who were determined not to be thrown/influenced by anything that might change their lives. Yellowstone was no match for them: sparkling air, ridge after ridge of lodgepole pine, a huge lake too cold to swim in, boiling rivers and snow in July; elk, bear, moose, bison, all watchfully guarding against too many intrusions into their property. And of course, water shooting 200 feet in the air against a gentian-blue sky, mudpots burping up hot gases and white-crusted earth grumbling and heaving beneath them. Our first camping trip was outside of the Park, north of the northern boundary, in an area that followed the Yellowstone River. Draining into the Yellowstone was a small tributary called Pine Creek. A well-used trail led through talus slopes and ultimately to the cold, clear waters of Pine Creek Lake, completely ringed by stone and sky. Bill had chosen this trail because it was steep but do-able, and because "There won't be any bears." Like most neophytes to Yellowstone, I was afraid of bears and not yet into the 'middle road' of the old timers: "Don't be afraid, but be cautious and know their behaviors." Of course, later I learned that bears didn't read the boundary signs: "You Are Now Out of the Park and into National Forest." But Bill felt this lie was a justifiable means to an end, the end being the discovery of the pristine mountain lake. We start out in the morning to cross Pine Creek on a huge fallen log that shifts as we balance across; the water is high this year. Then into woods that are wet year-round, mainly alpine fir. After the first few switchbacks, I can see where we are headed, and it's far away and high up. The sky is clouding over, which is typical of afternoons in this area--usually without rain and clearing again by sunset. But this looks stormier than usual, and clouds are rushing by and blackening furiously. "We're in for it," says Bill. At the edge of the stunted alpine vestiges of a forest, he gets out the pup tent. Camping with my dad, we had used folding cots and rigged tarps. I had never realized a pup tent was truly miniature size. The wind whips around, slapping the ropes in our faces, whipping our sleeping bags as we drag them in. The rain starts--huge, powerful drops that are not quite hail, but close. When I crawl in, I realize how tiny and dark this plastic coffin is, and I want, no, NEED, to get out. A strange new feeling envelops me: fear, panic, fracturing my thoughts, the deafening roar of driving buckets of rain hitting thin plastic, bending the canopy so Bill has to continually 'raise the roof' to dump buckets of water up and over onto the packed dirt and rocks. He laces up the entry and now starts to close the air vent at the other end where I am huddled, desperately looking out, seeing only more stormy darkness. "You can't do that!" I cry. "It's my only escape!" Bill shouts above the storm. "We can't leave it open. Let me tell you about hypothermia. We need to keep warm. Let’s change our socks from the wet creek and accumulate warmth in here. It's got to be shut." I realize what this panic is. For the first time in my life, I experience the full blown terror of claustrophobia. And no amount of pleading, no threats to bolt and stagger down the mountain, seem to change Bill's mind.

Then, he gets a brilliant idea. "Sue, tell me about the boyfriends in your life, starting from the first." (Now, I don't wish to imply that there were many, but the request covered a long span of time, so I am intrigued.) "Did I ever tell you about Bob? The high school I went to was 18 miles from my home, through the state forest where we lived, past a huge reservoir, through small northwest Connecticut towns, and Bob hitchhiked over to visit me one night. It was OK coming over, but at midnight nobody traveled that road. For our school's class night, he was given a pair of hiking boots ..." Well I am hooked, and on I go, shutting my eyes against the terror of the dark closing in, remembering times almost forgotten. Bill shouts against the storm, making appropriate comments to keep me going. And I traverse the years, starting to recount more recent points of interest. There is no answer. "Bill! Are you asleep?" Only the rain for an answer. So, where can I go now? What would keep my mind from being overwhelmed by panic? I start to sing: elementary school songs ("Ladybugs' Picnic"), guitar songs, lullabies I had used with my kids ("Hush, Little Baby"), hymns from a rousing evangelical Lutheran church ("Bringing in the Sheaves"), and others from a calmer locale ("A Mighty Fortress"), Bach Chorales. I find my voice, and am about to swing into my Requiem repertoire (Mozart, Brahms, Faure, Verdi) when the rain stops, the sky drips through widening patches of blue. Bill opens the air vent, and even the entryway, with great haste. (I have since wondered if the threat of "Then All Flesh Is Like the Grass" (Brahms) was the impetus for such speed? I am FREE. We leave the tent, bedraggled but upright (both the tent and us), pack up, and continue our climb in the eerie, wet, late afternoon light, using walking sticks to brace against the wet rocks. We arrive at Pine Creek Lake in time to sit among the boulders and see the sun color the evening with reds and oranges, reflecting into the freshly-washed, tiny sapphire lake. The downward trip is uneventful. Bill is exhausted after trying to manage his wife's phobias and I am gentled by pleasant memories.

We set up the pup tent, again, just as the colors fade, and this time go to sleep with all ports wide open. The next morning we discover the rain has washed every leaf, eroded the trail somewhat and roared down the creek at full speed. We get wet going across, knowing the sun and the car can be counted on to dry us out.

There is a moral to this story: the purpose of communication--speaking or singing-- is to help both talker and listener convey a sense of purpose. Or, when one gets to the Requiem singing, hopefully, a higher power will rescue you.

Chapter 25

Hike to Union Falls

William Britt Lewis, my son

These are my recollections of a hike my dad, William J. Lewis and I attempted some 46 years ago.

On my dad's lieu days while working as a ranger-naturalist in Yellowstone Park (a National Park Service euphemism for "days off" during the week), we would often go hiking or fishing as a family. Occasionally, a hike beyond the capabilities of the rest of the family was attempted. The following story recalls one of those hikes. I believe I was at most 12 years of age for this hike and possibly younger. I say this because I distinctly remember that we were living at the Old Faithful area when we departed and returned from the hike. Our family lived at the Norris Geyser Basin when I was 13, 14 and 15.

The Union Falls hike promised to be an interesting and scenic trip. According to the topographical maps, there were a number of waterfalls in the area and we planned to view them on the way to a unique waterfall--a confluence of two streams joining together in a waterfall and aptly named, Union Falls.

The terrain didn't appear too difficult to traverse, but at that time there was no trail to get to Union Falls. Such a hike would not be particularly unusual for us to attempt. We would have to cross the Falls River twice to get to Union Falls and back. Again, not too unusual as there are generally a lot of logs fallen across the streams and rivers in Yellowstone and we had scaled logs many times in the past. We knew that the hike would be 17-20 miles long, but I had previously hiked about 30 miles in a day.

To access the area, we drove out of Yellowstone through the South Entrance a few miles to Flagg Ranch where we headed west on the Reclamation Road; so named because it had been put in by the Bureau of Reclamation when the Grassy Lake Reservoir was built. It is now called the Grassy Lake Road. It ran more or less parallel to a very old homesteader's road, now for the most part lost to vegetation, called the St. Mary's Road.

Grassy Lake is an impoundment of Grassy Creek and empties into the Falls River upstream from our planned hiking area. It was built to capture the high water flows of spring snow melt and provide a reliable source of irrigation water for the many potato farms that commenced downstream at Ashton, Idaho and continued throughout the huge valley containing the Fall, Teton, Buffalo and Snake River drainages. The Reclamation Road is now a partially paved and mostly improved gravel road used primarily by tourists, but back in 1963 it was little more than an unmaintained jeep trail. Numerous turns, steep rises and erosion gullies crossing the track were its main features. I recall our Rambler station wagon hitting bottom several times as we crossed some of the deeper gullies that had logs thrown in them to make the road passable. The road runs roughly parallel to and south of the Southern boundary of Yellowstone and is only a few miles from Union Falls.

We found the spot where we would begin our hike about three miles west of Grassy Lake Reservoir where the road is within a few paces of Yellowstone's southern boundary and off through the forest we went to intersect the Falls River. On our way back from Union Falls, we planned to link up with a trail that led from within Yellowstone to the Grassy Lake. We were going to make a loop out of the hike so we could see as much of this new (to us) country as possible.

When we crossed Yellowstone's south boundary and reached the Falls River, we hiked downstream along its banks through a heavy forest, passing Cascade Acres and Terraced Falls. Today, there is a trail to these two features, but back in the '60s, we were on our own. As we were standing upon a bluff and cliff overlooking the river, the lens cap fell off my Dad's beloved Yashica 35mm camera and tumbled down the cliff. Despite the operative word "cliff", my Dad decided to attempt to retrieve the lens cap. I was instructed to remain where I was until Dad returned. After about 30 minutes, my concern grew and I started to see if there was a way for me to check on him. He then showed up with the lens cap but had lost his hat to the river after it was plucked off his head by a tree branch. Looking back, this was a harbinger of things to come.

Our plan was to follow the Falls River in a westerly direction until the landscape opened up in a wide valley on the West side of the Birch Hills, that were across the river from us. Then we would proceed north, crossing Proposition Creek and intersecting Mountain Ash Creek following it up to Union Falls. We had lost much time due to having to climb over lots of dead fall on our trail-less route plus the lens cap incident. The Falls River had also surprised us as to how big it was, so we decided to cross the river as soon as possible on fallen logs and forego visiting Rainbow Falls.

A crossing place of several trees forming a log jam presented itself and over the Falls River we went. We ate our lunch and headed north towards Union Falls on the east side of the Birch Hills, bushwhacking as we went. After a few hours of difficult hiking we decided that darkness was going to overtake us before we could get to Union Falls and back to the car. Plan 'C' consisted of our trying to bisect the trail that would take us back to Grassy Lake.

Without incident we turned east, found the trail and followed it to the Falls River crossing. The map had not indicated whether this crossing was bridged or if it consisted of a ford across the river. It turned out to be the latter and presented us with a daunting challenge. The ford would have been difficult and dangerous on horseback, let alone on foot. The river was running high as this was during the peak of irrigation season for the potato fields down river. The trail crossed at a very straight section of the river and it was simply a long wide deep stretch of rapids as far as we could see. I was getting pretty tired and darkness was descending upon us, so

Dad hiked up and down stream to try to find a suitable crossing. Long story short, that didn't happen.

The only other option available to us was to continue upstream along the river hoping to find a suitable crossing above the Grassy Lake confluence, then back to the Grassy Lake Reservoir dam and hike down the Reclamation Road to our car. It was a fair distance further for us as the river had many bends upstream (according to our map) and there was no trail. As dusk settled in, we decided that we would take the fastest route back to the car which meant fording the river.

There was an old snag that had fallen in the river on the opposite side from us. We couldn't use it to walk upon as it was mostly submerged, but we knew that if we were swept away in the current, there was a possibility, however remote, that we might catch ourselves on it. So upstream from the snag, a hundred or so feet, we began to cross the river. Perhaps I should note here that I was a very poor swimmer. Steadily, the river grew deeper. Dad clasped my hand and told me to stay alongside him on the downstream side so that he could break the swift force of the water as it pummeled us.

The rocks on the bottom were as slick as ice as the strong current had long ago washed away any sand or debris on the river bed. We were chest deep for my Dad and neck deep for me when I suddenly lost my footing and was swept downstream. Dad somehow retained his footing and held on to me as I was dangling at the end of his arm. He struggled to keep his own footing, stumbling a time or two as he reeled me back to his side. I don't remember the rest of the crossing very well, but somehow through grit and determination we made it across the river. I had been scared to death that we were both going to drown there, and if I wet myself, you would never know it as I was completely soaked from head to toe in water barely above freezing.

Onward we trudged along the trail with darkness and chilly temperatures closing in on us rapidly. It was only about four miles to our car but I was not able to walk at my usual pace and I was shivering uncontrollably. Dad put whatever extra wet clothing we had on me, including a heavy sweatshirt, but nothing could warm me up and I was weakening rapidly. We had never heard of the term hypothermia back then, but that's exactly what I had. Little did I realize that I was in a life-threatening state and minutes from death if I stopped moving. Dad had to cajole me to come along and he ended up dragging me by his side until we reached the dam at Grassy Lake in full darkness.

We planned to then follow the road to our car but we fortunately spotted a cabin where the summertime dam operator was housed. We pounded on the door for a few minutes before the operator opened it, as he assumed we were just tourists there to ask him some inane questions. However, as soon as he saw my condition, he gave me a candy bar, built a fire in his wood stove and perched me in front of it with a blanket. Poor Dad had to make the last three miles of the hike by himself to get the car.

After what seemed like forever, Dad returned, we thanked the dam operator for his assistance and headed for home. I vividly remember huddling on the floor of the Rambler Ambassador as close to the heater as I could get. Some two hours later, about midnight, we arrived at Old Faithful to a very worried wife and mother. I was still shivering, but put on some dry clothes and eventually warmed up.

Many of our neighbors at Old Faithful were fellow rangers and they were aware of our planned hike. Mom told us that the rangers had been checking for our return and that about 11 p.m., still not seeing that we had returned, they asked her if she wanted to send out a search party. We were glad to hear that there was concern for us and especially glad we didn't have to be rescued.

Well, that's the short version of the hike and I can honestly say that I have never had a desire to go see Union Falls again!

Chapter 26

Scatological Musings

My life as an interpreter at Yellowstone might have been rather routine if it weren't for some unusual experiences that occasionally spiced my existence. Here are three examples.

He arrived one summer to work in Yellowstone as a member of Student Conservation Association. "I'm from Boston. I've just finished my sophomore year in college and I'm looking for some experience as an interpreter", he told us. One day midway through the season, he was deemed ready to "fly solo" on a nature walk and I was asked to go along to give him some helpful suggestions at the conclusion. Part of the walk coursed through junipers and limber pines that had obviously served as shelter for a considerable number of mule deer. The SCA student gathered his group of park visitors and asked if they had been noticing all the "scat." A blonde, pony-tailed woman about 30 years old from California spoke up and asked, "What do you mean, scat?" He replied, "Oh, you know–all these droppings, these little pellets, this excrement." "Oh, you mean shit," she said. The leader flushed scarlet, drained to ashen ivory as then gasped, "Please watch your language. There are children present." He quickly moved the group to a new location. Thinking his words might have been irritating to the woman, I anonymously joined her as we walked along and commented, "He doesn't seem to like plain language." "Oh," she replied, "he wouldn't have thought anything about my language if he hadn't been from Boston [where people are more proper]."

While I'm not advocating that interpreters use words like "shit," I do believe that going to the other extreme is worse, as I heard one interpreter do as she told a group, "This is where the elk went to the bathroom." On another occasion I groaned as another interpreter referred to moose droppings as "do-do."

Most visitors, however, have been acculturated to believe that excrement is nasty, untouchable stuff. They gasp in sickened amazement whenever an interpreter picks up some dung, especially if the interpreter is female. And, yet, there's a fascination when the specimen is broken apart and its contents are analyzed. Finding hair in a coyote's dropping, tiny bones in an owl's pellet, or mostly grass in a grizzly's pile quickly demonstrate much about an animal's eating habits.

I frequently made weekly evening presentations at the Indian Creek Campground in Yellowstone Park with soil as my subject. I liked using materials from within a few feet of where my audience was seated on logs to illustrate a variety of things about the soil. Before the program I'd gather a couple of handfuls of elk pellets from the immediate area to demonstrate the movement of nutrients from the soil into plants, through animals and back to the soil. I'd break a dry winter elk dropping in two and show the group that it contained only dried grass. Then I'd pick up my gathered pellets, about the size of large olives, and toss them in the direction of the audience so they could feel and see for themselves. That got their attention. Many of them, probably for the first time in their lives, actually examined an animal dropping!

Chapter 27

Turning Negatives into Positives

I want to share with you an experience I had as a volunteer at the Park in the summer of 2007. First, however, I need to give you some background.

By my 34th summer in Yellowstone, alas, age had begun to take its toll. Glaucoma combined with macular degeneration began to reduce my visual acuity. I could no longer read without a magnifying aid. I was unable to see people's subtle facial expressions, that were so critical to understanding their responses to my critiques. This loss of vision (a severe negative) discouraged me from giving feedback to interpreters. So for several years I "retired" from giving what I had hoped were helpful suggestions. Still, my sense of hearing was excellent (a positive) and my vision wasn't "terrible" (I could still see the top three lines on the ophthalmologist's eye chart), and I could still go hiking by myself. So, for many summers, my wife (a positive) and I contented ourselves with interpreting for park visitors as volunteer hosts at the Museum of the National Park Ranger at the Norris Geyser Basin. When necessary, I found I could enlist the aid of a person to read descriptions and verify the right place on a map. I also discovered I could use other senses to compensate for my loss of vision. I could, for example, listen more carefully to the questions or comments (a positive). So, after years studying and teaching human communication, I was in the middle of a real-life communication experiment!

In 2007 so many retired rangers applied to be hosts at the Museum it was decided others needed to have the opportunity of hosting. We were notified we were “retired” (a negative). I called my friend, Katy Duffy, a supervisor located at the Old Faithful area. “Could you use my wife and me as volunteers this summer?” I asked. “Oh yes,” was the response. “You could rove through the geyser basins and explain the thermal features to people.” That's one of our favorite things to do and I readily agreed, but then she said, “What I <u>really</u> need you for, Bill, is training. I have six interpreters who are new to the Old Faithful area and some are just starting their work as interpreters.” “But I don't do training anymore,” citing my impaired vision. “I'll bet you can find a way.” (a positive) She was so persistent, I agreed to try (a positive). “How will I take notes? How will I remember what I want to suggest?” I thought to myself during the intervening months.

My first assignment was to help an interpreter with her guided walk at the Black Sand Basin. As I wrote my notes during her walk I could read as I wrote, but afterward as we began to talk, I discovered I could no longer read my writing. Fortunately, it was a memorable walk and I think I remembered most of what I wanted to tell her. As an example, my main suggestion was about the beginning of her walk. She had previously picked a spot to gather her group and had decided what she was going to say. About two minutes before the walk was scheduled to begin, a small geyser (15') began to explode with many bursts out of a pool about 50' away. When the time for the walk began, she gathered the group at the place she'd previously chosen and started telling them how long the walk was going to last, the distance it would cover, how they should be careful to stay on the walk, etc. I wanted her to move the group immediately to the geyser, saying something like, “I don't want you to miss seeing the geyser erupt up close. Let's go see what's happening!”

I was troubled by not being able to read my notes, so the second time I used block printing. “I'd surely be able to read that,” I said to myself. I also thought about using a recording device but decided it would be too distracting to the park visitors. When I sat down after the second walk I looked at my block-printed notes. Again, I couldn't read them! At that point, I had an inspiration! (a positive) I handed my notes to the new interpreter and asked, “Can you read my notes?” She could, and did. After she read aloud each remark I'd written, we talked about the comment. And so the session went. I felt it was one of the best feedback sessions in which I've participated. Why was that so? A couple of reasons have occurred to me. (1) We were both vulnerable. Each of us needed help and each of us gave it to the other. (2) Nothing was hidden. She saw all that I'd written. There were no secrets. So I've discovered a new and better way of giving a critique (a positive). It worked for me.

Sometimes vision doesn’t make any difference. A touching moment occurred while my wife and I were volunteering at the Museum of the National Park Ranger. It was the end of the day and time to lower the American flag from the pole. There was a group there with kids, and, as usual we asked the kids for help taking down the flag. They always jumped right in with enthusiasm. There was a family with us from Korea who had recently been granted citizenship. The eight-year-old son assisted me in lowering and folding the flag. As we looked past the flag into the Gibbon Meadow, under a cloudless, deep blue sky, we saw a herd of bison grazing in the distance. His family was soon in tears. What a thrilling moment for all of us!

Chapter 28

The Last Hurrah

Since I'm still a young person hiding in an eighty-plus-year-old body, for many summers since officially retiring I've been going back to Yellowstone to serve as a volunteer doing training for the interpretive staff at Old Faithful. As 2009 rolled around, I decided the time had come to really retire, "one last time." Age-related macular degeneration and glaucoma had weakened my vision to near-blindness and this made getting around too difficult. Since I was going to be in the Yellowstone area visiting my two Montana sons and their families, I agreed to do a training session "one more time."

My long-time friend and host at Old Faithful, Katy Duffy, arranged a potluck around a campfire and invited about twenty people to participate. Ominous clouds joining over our gathering place spat us indoors where we enjoyed Katy's cozy living room. When the meal concluded, the training began. I gave each participant a piece of paper (recycled, of course) and told them I was going to play some recorded music for them and asked them to write what went through their minds as they listened: thoughts and mental pictures, whether they liked it or not, the name of the piece, whether they would play this at home, etc. The first cut was on a vinyl record called "Beatles Baroque", but I didn't announce it. All of the tunes on the record were originally written by the Beatles, but they were now played in classical baroque style. After playing the piece, I gathered all the papers, shuffled and redistributed them. Then each person was asked to read the paper they held. "Sounds like a formal dance." "I see powdered wigs, pantaloons, and ball gowns." "It's music I don't like." "It's formal and strident." Then I told them they had heard a Beatles tune, "I Want to Hold Your Hand" played in baroque style. (I thought that even though the song is old it is still well known.) "No, that can't be!" "That's ridiculous." "No way", they said. So I played part of the original tune as the Beatles had played it. Again, there was disbelief. I told the group I would play the baroque version again and this time I'd help them hear the melody hidden in the baroque version. I sang the Beatles' refrain whenever it appeared. Now they got it! "That's not what I heard the *first* time !" "What's the difference?" Now they knew what to look for. What had previously been 'hidden' was now apparent. They'd been helped to go beyond their first impressions. They had evidently experienced something in a new way.

After making this presentation and returning home to Vermont, I received the following note from Katy Duffy:

> *Dear Bill,*
>
> *I want you to know that the interpreters who came to meet you in September felt as if they were on a pilgrimage to meet, learn from and be inspired by their hero–YOU! Your gentle style and relevant stories helped these young interpreters to believe they have chosen the right profession. You have a knack for empowering your listeners, making it easy for them to develop their skills and abilities to be effective interpreters. Everything you said and did reinforced the importance of the role interpreters play in connecting park visitors with Yellowstone's wonders. Every interpreter, including Butch (Senior Seasonal Interpreter at Old Faithful) and me, at the end of the night felt privileged to have been in your presence. You have a calming and uplifting influence on your listeners. We are grateful to you!*

I sincerely believe that both good learning and good teaching are based on a shared curiosity, joy and an openness to new experiences. I hope this book inspires you to look at life in new ways.

Appendix A

An Autobiographical Sketch of the Author

I was born in 1923 in the farming community of Twin Groves, Idaho, in the southeastern part of the state near the Yellowstone and Grand Teton National Parks. My father was a schoolteacher and principal of a two-room schoolhouse, where he hauled water from the canal that ran nearby and kept the woodstove going. My parents lived in the schoolhouse in an apartment adjacent to the classrooms. I was my parents' first child and was born in their apartment, my mother being assisted by a doctor who came to the house. When I was in second grade my family moved to nearby St. Anthony, Idaho where my father owned a grocery store for many years.

In the early years, we had no running water or electricity. My mother was a singer and talented "reader", who performed dramatic readings of stories and poems at small gatherings. She valued education very much and passed that along to me.

My first work for pay was as a clerk in my father's grocerystore where I stocked shelves, waited on customers and learned from the butcher how to cut meat off the bones and make hamburger. The store was a family enterprise so I didn't make very much money. My first regular paying job was with the Northrup King Seed Company, which contracted with farmers to grow peas for seed in the Upper Snake River Valley. I had just completed my junior year in high school (1941) and was delighted to have a job with regular wages since I had to pay for college myself. My job was to walk up and down the rows of peas and pull up the plants, called rogues, that were not of the variety wanted. As I was working, my eyes often rose to the magnificent mountain peaks of the Grand Teton National Park, easily visible from where I was.

This was the start of my love for the land and nature, that only grew deeper with the years to come.

My career with the federal government began the following summer (1942) when I was hired as a "laborer" with the Forest Service in the Targhee National Forest. The crew to which I was assigned was given the task of building a telephone line from near Pond's Lodge to a fire lookout tower on the top of Mt. Sawtell. This was for the purpose of fire reporting. Previously, radio had been used, but it was not reliable. Hence, our labor was needed to set up telephone communication. With our five man crew we did a lot of tree and brush cutting, digging holes, putting poles in and hanging the line. I became adept at climbing poles and trees as well as working with crosscut saws and double-edged axes. Since we were working with the telephone line all the time, we were always connected. When a fire broke out, we heard about it and were the first crew on it. By the end of the summer we'd fought eight fires. Now "experienced", three of us were each assigned a group of ten men between 25 and 45 years old to supervise. To be 17 years old and in charge of a crew of older men felt a little strange for us. But we knew how to fight fires and it worked out well.

In the fall I enrolled at Brigham Young University. I met my expenses with what I'd earned from my work with the Forest Service plus a new job in Provo, Utah as an assistant manager of the Strand movie theatre, earning .25/hour. As my room and board cost $25/month and tuition cost $75 per year, I had money to spare.

One day while working at the Strand, the Japanese bombed Pearl Harbor. The projectionist stopped the film and asked me to inform the audience of this momentous event. After my announcement, half of the viewers, realizing the horror of this surprise attack, left the theatre.

After Pearl Harbor, I decided I'd better join one of the military services before I was drafted and had no choice of service. I was still at Brigham Young University, and I joined the Navy V-12 program that allowed servicemen to remain in college as long as they were studying a subject that was "vital" to the interests of the U.S. and at a college of their choosing. The Navy would pay tuition, living expenses and a small allowance for up to four semesters. So I left for my second federal experience, this time as a seaman at the University of New Mexico at Albuquerque and pursued a major in electrical engineering. I studied hard and did a lot of marching!

After four semesters at the University of New Mexico, the Navy sent me off to Columbia University in New York City to learn how to be a Midshipman, that meant an increase in pay and status. At the end of four months I was commissioned as an Ensign, another pay increase, and was sent to Harvard to be trained as an officer with a specialty in communication. Then 22 years old, I was assigned to the USS Shamrock Bay, an aircraft carrier where I spent most of my time decoding messages, supervising, and working on equipment. I served for three years in the Pacific and Atlantic before being discharged as a Lt. j.g. (ie: junior grade)

My active duty with the Federal Government having ended, I took a new direction. As a recipient of the G.I. Bill, I was financially able to receive a B.A. degree at Brigham Young University, an M.A. at Northwestern University, and a Ph.D. at the University of Florida. With my degrees in hand, I began an academic career as a faculty member at Ohio University (three years), Penn State University (one year) and the University of Vermont (30 years). As an academician, I had my summers “free”. What to do? I needed a summer job to help meet the financial needs of a growing family and I had to be busy. My mind turned West as I remembered that one of my favorite high school teachers and debate and drama coach, Alton B. Jones, had worked as a seasonal park ranger in the Grand Teton National Park. His stories had always interested me. And my parents, brother and sisters were there. My roots were there. I’d camped in Yellowstone National Park at the age of five and later visited the Park several times growing up. Once in high school, a friend and I pedaled our one-gear, balloon tire bicycles to the Park and back, about 150 miles round trip--no titanium 21-speed bikes for us!

I decided to apply to Yellowstone for a summer job as a temporary park ranger and was hired in 1949 starting out as a Government Service-3 (GS-3), a very low rank. There was a problem however: they had a position for me but no housing. I had a wife and a two-year-old daughter. Before accepting the job, I discussed the dilemma with my parents' next door neighbors in St. Anthony, Idaho, about 75 miles away. The father had a house trailer he wasn't using that summer and asked if I would like to use it. I was flabbergasted at his offer, but even more so when he said he would attach it to his pickup truck and haul it to Yellowstone. The Park agreed to this plan and gave us an electrical connection but no running water. So we carried water all summer and learned to use an outhouse.

The job to which I was assigned included patrolling the Old Faithful area, on foot and in a car, making sure the pools and geysers were protected from people throwing objects into them, scratching their names into the colorful bacterial growths in the thermal runoff channels, removing specimens, etc. My responsibilities also included protecting park visitors from the thermal features, which can be dangerous. When my superiors learned of my skill with a typewriter I was put in the office and asked to type reports, respond to radio messages and run the office when no one else was there.

During my second summer I was assigned more and more to running the Communication Center. The Park offered us a variety of housing after that first year, including two small, one-room log cabins across a dirt road from each other. We slept in one cabin and ate in the other. Still we had to haul our water, but this location featured a two-holer outhouse! My daughter, Kathy, tells me now that she was always embarrassed to use it, fearing that someone would come in and occupy one of the holes while she was on the other. In subsequent years our housing was upgraded to an apartment and then a house.

The following year the Fishing Bridge area needed someone full-time to run their Communication Center, and I was assigned to do it. I enjoyed it, but I didn't go to Yellowstone to work inside a building. I asked to be transferred to the Interpretive Division where I could do walks, hikes, evening campfire talks, and answer questions in the visitor center. I was reassigned to the Old Faithful area, where I spent many happy summers. I was also given "career conditional" status, which means that you work for a summer and are then furloughed for the rest of the year. This was very important because it allowed me to keep my academic job the rest of the year, and made me eligible for a federal retirement pension.

One summer I was at Old Faithful when some remarkable geyser activity began 30 miles north at the Norris Geyser Basin. One of its geysers, Steamboat Geyser, suddenly became the highest geyser in the world. Small rocks and superheated water were exploding with a roar to 300 feet at unpredictable and infrequent intervals. Nearby was the Echinus Geyser, which (for the first time) started to erupt from a pool of superheated water. To my delight I was transferred there. I assisted in managing the large numbers of visitors now coming to see the geysers.

Then a life-changing event occurred at my job at the University of Vermont. The Chairman of my department decided to take a sabbatical leave and wanted me to be acting chairman for the next 12 months. "I can't do that. I go to Yellowstone every summer." "But you're the only one I want to lead the department while I'm gone." "But I have a career-conditional arrangement that I'll lose if I don't go back each year." "How long do you have to be there to maintain your status?" I checked and found the minimum time was three weeks. "How about asking Yellowstone to see if they'll take you for that period?" I did and Yellowstone was willing. Now they had to decide out how to use me. I had been involved in training interpreters in communication skills at Old Faithful and Norris Geyser Basin. So it was decided that they'd use me to run a group training session for all of the interpreters in the park, about 50 people, and then to train them individually. I'd go on a walk, take notes, and sit down with the interpreter afterward and give helpful feedback. My supervisors thought this turned out so well that the following summer they created the position of chief park critiquer for me and had me doing communication training all through the park. I was promoted to a GS-7 and I worked independently out of park headquarters at Mammoth Hot Springs. I held that position for ten years.

Word got to NPS headquarters in Washington D.C. and they sent a representative to Yellowstone to observe this new endeavor. On-the-spot critiquing worked. The representative came to observe, videotaped me at work and took it back to Washington D.C. When he showed the tape to headquarters, the decision was made to make an interpretive training video for use throughout the National Park System. I was videotaped critiquing interpreters and the resulting video, *The Process of Interpretive Critiquing*, has been widely used for training staff in parks and museums throughout the United States, England and Canada. The NPS then sent me to give trainings in person in many interpretive settings in most of the 50 states. Later I wrote a manual for interpreters, *Interpreting for Park Visitors*, (1981) and it is still in print today (2010) in several languages.

In the meantime Yellowstone decided my work deserved more pay than I was making. When they asked the personnel office how to go about this, they replied, "You can't raise his pay, but you could promote him, and from your description of his job, he's doing work at a higher level."

Thus, the question, "What'll we do with Bill Lewis for three weeks?" led to a videotape on training, a book on interpretation, and now to this book, not to mention a very interesting and fulfilling career!

Appendix B

Communication Principles

The principles of communication in this book came from the following beliefs that I've distilled from my experiences.

Concepts

1. We all bring our past to the present.
2. Categories can blind us.
3. First impressions are especially important.
4. Unless helped, we often fail to find, see, comprehend.
5. Meanings are in people, not words.
6. My perception is not your perception.
7. Circuit overload causes distortion and fatigue.
8. Feedback is essential.
9. Simplicity and organization clarify messages.
10. A picture can be worth a thousand words.

Learning Principles

1. People learn better when they're actively involved in the learning process.
2. People learn better when they're using as many senses as appropriate.

3. People prefer to learn that which is of most value to them at the present.
4. That which people discover for themselves generates a special and vital excitement and satisfaction.
5. Learning requires activity on the part of the learner.
6. Friendly competition stimulates learning.
7. Knowing the usefulness of the knowledge being acquired makes learning more effective.
8. People learn best from hands-on experience.
9. People learn best when the experience is close to them in time and space.
10. Questions can be effectively used to help people derive meanings.
11. Giving people expectations at the beginning of an activity will focus attention and improve learning.
12. The ways in which people are responded to affects their learning.

To communicate effectively with a group:

1. Be prepared.
2. Let people know who you are.
3. Find out and adapt to the uniqueness of the group.
4. Involve your listeners. How does your information relate to their lives?
5. Give them what they want.
6. Talk about what is happening in the small world that is around you now. Use spontaneous events readily.
7. Avoid apologies.

Acknowledgments

Every summer from 1949 to about 1973 my first wife, Bobby Jean Watson, made the trek from Vermont to Yellowstone with me and our four children as they came along. The eldest two, Kathy and Britt, have contributed chapters to this book. The other two, Jim and Roger, read drafts and made helpful comments.

I introduced my second wife, Suzanne Kusserow, to Yellowstone in 1979 and we spent many happy summers there. As the years have passed, she has heard me tell many stories about Yellowstone, and finally suggested that I should publish them as a book. She has included one of her own stories in which she describes her fears of camping with bears. She encouraged me to keep writing throughout the two years of this project and did considerable editing.

Because of my poor vision, I wrote this book long-hand using an enlarger, an optical device that magnifies the printed word onto a lighted screen. I then handed it over to Jana Fabri Sbardellati, who has read to me almost every week for 10 years. She typed the entire first draft from my rather cryptic long-hand and has worked hard helping to edit it. Chief editor was Sandy Lord who labored long and diligently to make the book hang together in a clear and intelligent way.

Among the permanent National Park Supervisors who helped my seasonal efforts are Alan Mebane, Stan Canter, Bill Dunmire, Roy Graybill, Frank Kowski, Katy Duffy, and Riley McClelland. Others who helped me are Butch (Orville) Bach, Sam Holbrook, Alan Leftridge, Ellen Frost, George Algard, Guida Veronda, and Jean Falbo.

www.ingramcontent.com/pod-product-compliance
Ingram Content Group UK Ltd.
Pitfield, Milton Keynes, MK11 3LW, UK
UKHW020240250726
13967UKWH00001B/474